Notes from the Equestrian Underground

Carol Frey

NOTES FROM THE EQUESTRIAN UNDERGROUND

Copyright @ 2015 by Carol Frey Yingling. All rights reserved. Printed in the United States of America. No part of this book may be used or reproduced in any manner whatsoever without written permission except in the case of brief quotations embodied in critical articles or reviews. For information, address Carol.Yingling@gmail.com.

www.carol-frey.com

Thanks go out to….

- a lot of friends, riders and non-riders alike, who may possibly have inspired some of these fictional adventures. (If you think you recognize yourself, and you are offended, then it wasn't you. Really. But if you're happy about it, maybe you are the inspiration.)

- the Beehive Queen, who originally coaxed the Underground from a sea of emails.

- my friend John A. Stewart and the Amity Art Foundation, who provided energy and advice along with the belief that art of all types makes the world a better place.

- and especially to my husband, sons, parents, extended family and friends who have shared the many real-life adventures of the Equestrian Underground!

Notes from the Equestrian Underground

Because moms begin as someone else and assume other identities after motherhood. Eventually.

CONTENTS

PROLOGUE 11

THE BEGINNING
MY FIRST (REAL) RIDE 17
MR. NORTON: MASCULINE IDEAL 19
MY FIRST HORSE: DEATH OF A FANTASY 23
A CONVENIENT PRESCRIPTION 29
TOYING WITH ME: HORSE IN THE ROAD 36

LOVE
BIG: HIGH SPIRITS 43
TV FANTASY HORSES 48
PONYTAIL BOB GOT HIS MARBLES 53
QUESTION'S FAVORITE HUMAN 58
SKI LIFTS AND SPORTS BRAS 62
SCHOONER HAS A BALL 71
CREATIVE USE OF A TACK TRUNK 79
IN MEMORIAM: SCHOONER 83

HORSE SHOWS
RESERVE CHAMPIONS OF SOMETHING 93
AMBITION: HOW I WANT TO RIDE 103
AGING GRACEFULLY 107

COMPETITIVE BY NATURE 111
THE PROFESSIONAL 116
RULES OF A SHOW: HOW TO BREAK THEM 119
ON THE SIDE OF THE ROAD 123

DRESSAGE
A SYNCOPATED RHYTHM 137
RELAXATION 143
CONNECTION 149
IMPULSION 154
STRAIGHTNESS 157
COLLECTION 161

LESSONS LEARNED
TRAINING SAM 169
TRICKSTER 174
JOSEPHINE AND HER CURE 177
CONFIDENCE 181
REX RIDES! 195
DIFFERENT JOBS 199
SHOPPING? UGH! 205
LEAP OF FAITH 222
ENGLISH AS A SECOND LANGUAGE 227
GENEROSITY 231

LIFE AROUND THE BARN
AND THROUGH THE WOODS 237

THANKFUL FOR BARN CATS	243
BARN FOOD	248
CHICKLETTE GAMES	252
COOL BLUE STEEL: 194 HORSES	255
FIREWORKS	263
FIREWORKS: PREPARATION	267
NAME CHANGE	271
PHONE CALLS	276
REVENGE OF THE PHONE CALLS	280
EVEN MORE PHONE CALLS	283
TIME FOR A BARN IN MY BACKYARD	286
EPILOGUE	295

PROLOGUE
BACK IN THE SADDLE, LITERALLY

So the boys got me riding lessons for Christmas. They were trying to interest me in a new hobby, obviously. Bing's ill-concealed attempt to distract me from telling stories about the family (and publishing them) hadn't fooled me in the least. The other gifts - a decoupage kit (seriously? Fussy painting and artistic talent required? What were they thinking?), a tennis racquet (no way am I baring my crepe-y thighs - I'll take up tennis again when it's played in bloomers), calligraphy pens (once again, artistic talent is required, so it's not an option) - were stacked in a closet. Way in the back. But riding lessons... I'd always loved horses, had ridden while growing up in the Midwest... maybe...

I made the arrangements. I wore lightweight hiking boots, with a heel. I got a helmet. And I panicked.

Long, long ago, in sixth grade, I'd been given riding lessons for Christmas. I joined a class of nine beginners, all sitting tentatively on bored horses who shuffled around the ring. Since I loved horses so much, I figured I'd be a natural rider. I'd had pony lessons before I could read, I reasoned, and, speaking of reading, I'd read every single book on horses in the public and school libraries. I bought horse magazines whenever I could. I would ride like a star.

I rode like a warthog. All my reading and prior (and limited) experience was with a big, sturdy Western saddle - the ones with a handle that cowboys use to hold rope while they're subduing cows, and the rest of us use to stay on the horse. This was an English riding stable. The saddles were flat. There weren't any handy places to grab when panicked. The saddle didn't have comforting bumps to securely cradle my rear.

When the class was asked to trot, I began to bounce. It was uncomfortable. I tried to relax and control my bouncing. I tried to remember what the instructor had said. I tried to hear what the instructor was currently saying. But mostly, I tried not to bounce too much on my rapidly bruising bottom.

"You!" the instructor bellowed, pointing at me. "Nice job posting!"

I had no idea what she was talking about, but I grinned. I was riding like a star after all! At least I thought so, until my third lesson.

I had no idea what I was doing. I was bouncing around on a long-suffering lesson horse after only two lessons, but the instructor had praised my posting, whatever "posting" is. So my sixth-grade self was feeling like the star I had planned on being.

And then I was told to "drop my stirrups." A little further instruction, and I understood that meant to take my feet out of the stirrups.

They did not go over this in the Western riding magazines I'd been reading.

But I gamely followed along with the class, urged my Standardbred mare to trot, and, within a minute and a half, fell off.

I rode like a warthog after all.

And now this warthog, thirty-plus years later, was going to take another riding lesson. Meanwhile, I had ridden hundreds of miles as a teenager on my trusty Sam, mostly bareback, had fallen off countless times, and I had some hope of remembering... something. I had visited the barn where I would ride with my girlfriend Shelly, who had recently acquired a horse, and I'd fallen back in love with all things equine. But this time I knew mere passion did not a rider make - lots and lots of practice was needed, too.

With great trepidation, I climbed the mounting block like it was a scaffold and prepared for public humiliation. Thirty minutes later, I slid off the impressively patient chestnut gelding and couldn't stop grinning.

Hooked. I was definitely hooked.

THE BEGINNING

In every cowgirl's life there is that moment when she touches her first horse and the course of her life is forever changed.
        – Wildflower Cowgirl

MY FIRST (REAL) RIDE

I can't remember not loving horses. When I was a preschooler, in a place long ago and far away, my parents hired an old man to haul away a downed apple tree. He used an enormous wagon and his two-horse team. My parents let me ride in the wagon with him. The horses swished their amazingly coarse tails, brushing against my bare knees and arms. They pooped, and they sweated, and they smelled and attracted flies. And I was fascinated.

Not long after, my family went to a little fair. There was a pony ride. Today, large barns buy these contraptions that walk horses to cool them out or condition them. They cost thousands of dollars. But, in this place long ago and far away, there was a relatively inexpensive contraption much like a modern hot walker that kept five or six ponies walking so that little kids could ride them. That was my first ride.

The fuzzy little Shetland was chocolate brown and totally unimpressed by my adoration. My parents paid for a ride for me, and I knew bliss. And then, after a few minutes, the pony stopped. All the ponies stopped.

The ride was over. My parents came to me to take me off the chocolate brown pony. Who had become my equine soulmate, and I had named him "Brownie."

The story that my parents tell has me throwing a fit of such magnitude that they bought me another pony ride. I know, in my heart, that what really happened is that Brownie pitched a fit at the first hint of losing the rider that he knew was his Velvet Brown, the Lone Ranger to his Silver, the Roy Rogers to his Trigger. My parents, and the owner of the ponies and the ride, astonished at the unbreakable bond so quickly developed, allowed us to continue our ride. The only thing that separated us was the lack of imagination on the part of my parents: they could have traded my little brother for Brownie.

But they didn't even try.

MR. NORTON: MASCULINE IDEAL

After I'd ridden a mechanical horse – or several - courtesy of my indulgent grandfather, and then a real, live pony at a fair courtesy of my indulgent parents, I began to campaign for a pony of my own. My parents started to cave... and somehow I began getting riding lessons from a local farmer named Mr. Norton. How that started, and exactly when, and even where this magical farm was located is all a fuzzy memory to my parents. They don't even remember Mr. Norton's name. But his name, his face, and especially his ponies, are among my favorite memory treasures.

This was in the Midwest. In a little town, long ago. It was a far cry (a really long yodel, even) from the tall boots and velvet hunt caps of the East Coast pony clubs or the dusty plains and sagebrush of the cowboy West.

Mr. Norton owned a little working farm with cows, chickens, and three ponies: two fat and furry yellow

Shetlands named Hopalong and Speedy and an emphatically opinionated grey Welsh he called Mike. I insisted the Shetlands were twins because I couldn't tell them apart. My mother, a horsewoman in her own right, tried to tell me that they were brothers, but not twins. I refused to believe her, because I was even more opinionated than the pony named Mike.

Mr. Norton agreed with me. Looking back, I suspect he found a stubborn little girl with russet ringlets and a pronounced pout amusing, in weekly doses. At the time, however, I was sure that he recognized a fellow horse person, and that we understood each other as only the elite who truly love all things equine could.

His idea of riding included clinging to the horn on a Western saddle whenever necessary ("What's it there for, eh?") and making sure my right hand was free so I'd be able to take up lasso swinging once I mastered riding. Mr. Norton also taught me to lean forward to ride under trees.

I loved doing that. It was so practical, and made so

much sense, and I could do it (unlike lasso swinging, which I practiced diligently and unsuccessfully with a length of clothesline). On the lesson day closest to my birthday, Mr. Norton let me ride Speedy in the small pasture unsupervised. Sort of. He stood at the top of the small rise and watched me, but did not correct my riding. He let me choose where to go. I circled through the little patch of woods repeatedly so I could lean forward to duck under the one branch overhanging the path. This was Mr. Norton's birthday gift to me: an independent ride and the illusion of freedom. It thrilled me as no doll or plastic toy ever did.

One day the Shetland I was riding ran away with me. He ran through a flock of chickens that had been pecking away in one corner of the small pasture. They scattered, squawking and shedding feathers, as Hopalong thundered among them. I cried and cried.

Mr. Norton soothed me, chuckling softly at my tears until I stopped sobbing about killing his fluffy hens. He reassured me that they were fine, there were no limp and feathery bodies - in fact, they were clucking and scratching contentedly as though nothing had happened. And he praised me for staying on, calling me a real cowgirl.

He wore overalls and chewed pieces of hay or grass. He spoke slowly and gently. His face had leathered from the sun, and he squinted beneath a cap disreputable with age and dust.

Mr. Norton had ponies and he let me ride them. Therefore he is ever The Perfect Man, my version of The Masculine Ideal. I loved him, and still do.

Rex squints. And Rex bought my mare Bea for me. He reminds me of Mr. Norton.

MY FIRST HORSE: DEATH OF A FANTASY

I wanted a horse since I was born, and possibly before. When my mother reminisces about my pre-birth kicking (she claims I was very active), I tell her I was trying to add leg and encourage her forward. She is much less amused by this than I am, although I think it is only the implication that she moved slowly that offends her.

For my thirteenth birthday, my parents relented and told me I could have a horse. The pieces had fallen in place: we lived in a (very) small Midwestern town surrounded by farms; my gregarious mother had befriended the Corn Man who sold produce door-to-door from the trunk of his red Mustang and kept horses, including a couple of boarders; they were tired of me mooning over horse books in my room and asking to decorate it like a stall (some pre-teens played with Barbie dolls, I played with horses and threw a Barbie into the mix once in a while, trying to wedge the unbending doll onto a plastic horse's back).

The Corn Man, Mr. Johnson, was a retired cowboy who liked horses and appreciated teenagers. He and his wife lived in a small house on the farm they shared with their older son, who lived in the big old farmhouse on the other side of the driveway. They had a couple of enormous pastures fenced in with miles of barbed wire, and one of these twelve-acre paradises housed a small herd of various equines. To which my new horse would be added, at a yearly cost of less than one month's board at an Eastern stable with English saddles and amenities like bathrooms.

My father took me horse shopping. Neither of us knew anything beyond what I read in books and what Dad read in his checkbook. This being long before the internet, I scoured the classified ads every day. We went to brokers, and one horse, a chestnut mare named "Sunday Sue," proved easy for me to ride, responsive and tame. And then she started coughing, and the broker magically produced a syringe and deftly injected her in the neck, telling me that it was no problem. We did not buy Sunday Sue. One owner had two horses for sale. The blue roan was interesting, and I was so excited to go there that I wore two different shoes (not paddock boots, but two different shoes with heels). The blue roan did not want to leave the rawboned sorrel, and protested our short ride down the driveway. Energetically. We did not buy the blue roan, or the rawboned sorrel. Another broker kept a small group of horses in a large enclosed ring. One, a very young, extremely cute bay gelding, was for sale at the right price. I rode him, then went back several days later and rode him again. At this point, I was enjoying the shopping. Dad wasn't. He and the broker talked while I patted the little bay.

Dad came over to me.

"Do you like this one?" he asked.

"Yeah... I guess... " I said, considering a bit.

"You think he'd make a nice horse for you?"

"Probably," I replied, still considering.

Dad walked away and I rearranged Small Bay Horse's forelock, which was thick and unruly. When Dad returned, we'd bought the horse.

I was stunned. I didn't think I'd agreed to this. I'd had a fantasy. My horse was going to look at me and claim me as his human. We'd form an immediate, undying partnership. Only I would be able to ride him. He would be magnificent, and large, and probably black. Maybe white, or dappled grey. Small Bay Horse was a reality, and I was still looking for my fantasy.

Two days later, after the check for one-half of Small Bay Horse cleared, he was delivered to Mr. Johnson's farm. Dad and Mom were more excited than I was. Dad named the horse Saturday Sam, as a nod to the gentle but coughing Sunday Sue. I remained shocked, but gamely visited Sam daily and rode, and groomed, and petted him.

I eventually grew to love him dearly, and he eventually fulfilled some of my fantasies. Sam didn't let others ride him, but instead of rearing in magnificent protest, he stood still and turned his head to watch the unfamiliar rider kicking and clucking and waving sticks to try to get him to move. Sam came to me when he saw me in the pasture. He didn't scream and rear and run to me like my fantasy horse, he just looked up at my call and ambled in my general direction, sometimes even stopping for a quick bite from a particularly enticing patch of clover. Sam also let me hop on him, bareback, first with a halter and lead rope and then with just a rope, and ride him through two gates and out of the pasture. This had never been on my list of fantasies, but, years later, it was good for bragging. Whenever a famous trainer was credited with being so in touch with his horse that he could open - and close! - gates from the saddle, I snickered unattractively. I opened and closed gates from atop Sam without a saddle and bridle, with no more than a lead rope circling his neck.

Of course, if I tried to ride Sam from the pasture without at least that lead rope around his neck, he ambled over to the nearest tree, calmly ignoring anything I did, and gently scraped me off. I guess he thought I should put some effort into our partnership.

One of the things I learned from Sam and our arranged partnership was that it's scary to commit because it ends the fantasies. I didn't get The Black Stallion, or Flame, or Fury, or Silver, or Trigger, or any of the other famous - and unlikely - horses. I found a partner who carried me through my teen years and deposited me, at eighteen, on the brink of adulthood and went on to graciously carry another young girl through her own turbulent teen years. And I'll always hold tender memories of Sam, that Small Bay Not Quite My Fantasy Horse.

A CONVENIENT PRESCRIPTION

My dentist is a big part of my life. I have a lot of dental work, and I've known Dr. Marc longer than I've known Rex. Sadly, Rex is also Dr. Marc's patient and they conspired, a couple of years ago, to keep me from getting a gold cap on one of my molars. I thought it would give me an interesting, flashy smile. And it would only show when I grinned really big. They thought I was having trouble with "the change." I almost changed dentists, but then Dr. Marc redeemed himself…

I was relaxing during one of my regularly scheduled cleanings (if I neglect my teeth, they will protest and break on cucumbers and oatmeal, and I'll end up with another root canal, so I'm pretty disciplined on scheduling dentist visits and catching problems before my ridiculously soft teeth crumble). Dr. Marc came in after the nice hygienist had me swish and spit for the last time. He poked around for a while, and spoke with the hygienist in low tones.

"Receding gums," he said, in a voice of doom. Of

course, almost anything said in a dentist's office sounds like the voice of doom.

"Yes," she answered, and spouted some sort of technical sounding jargon involving millimeters and pockets.

Dr. Marc stopped probing and stood up. "You have receding gums," he said.

"Uh-huh," I responded. I had figured that out from his first comment.

He waited. Obviously I needed to react.

"Is there anything I can do?" That seemed like a good question.

"No. Later we can treat it." He looked cheerful. Did he have a new boat? A new house by the beach? In Aruba?

"What causes it?" I asked, figuring maybe I could

handle it before I had gum surgery, which I had a vague idea involved knives and needles and stitches – and pain.

Dr. Marc bent over me again and put fingers and an implement in my mouth. "Oh, age, and heredity."

Not enough of an answer. I gurgled at him in a questioning tone.

He shrugged. "And stress," he added.

I made the magic sign. He and I had agreed on a gesture to make him get out of my mouth several years ago. He didn't want me to bite or scream, and I was afraid to hit him, or even touch him, in case he flinched while holding something sharp in my mouth.

Dr. Marc backed out of my mouth. He knew screaming and biting was my failsafe if he did not comply.

"I want a prescription for stress," I told him. I'd had a few horseback riding lessons and wanted to continue.

This looked like an opportunity, not a problem.

"Yes?" Did I mention he's known me longer than Rex has? He waited for the punch line. I sometimes begged for Novocaine, but had never begged for anything else from Dr. Marc. He was understandably suspicious, and showed it, narrowing his eyes behind his mad-scientist magnifying spectacles.

"I want a prescription for riding lessons," I said.

"Wouldn't you rather to go to a spa?" he asked.

"No. I like to horseback ride. And I want a prescription to give to Rex."

"Wouldn't you rather go shopping?" Dr. Marc suggested. He was obviously confused.

"No," I said. "I want to shop for riding lessons."

"Wouldn't you rather have your nails done? Horses are big and dirty and smelly. You could get a manicure and pedicure instead." Obviously Mrs. Dr. Marc has different priorities than I do.

"Seriously? No."

Dr. Marc laughed and returned to poking around in my mouth some more, grinning. After he and the hygienist murmured a few more things, I was relieved of my now-nasty little paper bib and released. As I exchanged pleasantries with the nice receptionist, who has a higher-than-average rate of return calls because she's so friendly and no one wants to disappoint her, Dr. Marc came dashing from his office, waving a prescription slip.

It stated, in barely readable dentist scrawl, "For treatment of gingival recession and stress. Weekly riding lessons. As directed." And it was signed. It was official.

That night, I put it on the refrigerator under one of the many ugly magnets advertising plumbers and electricians that have long since retired. When Rex came home, he cheerfully asked me how my dentist appointment went.

"OK… " I answered and bit my lip, looking downcast.

"What happened?" he asked, instantly concerned. Rex is a good guy.

"I got a prescription… it's pretty expensive."

"Will our insurance cover it?"

"No."

"Are you sure?"

"Yes. It's for my receding gums. It's not a life-threatening situation, and it's a pretty expensive prescription."

"If you need it, we'll get it," Rex said, loyally. He's so nice. I shouldn't be so tough on him. Sometimes I think I really should hate myself, but I get over it.

I waved to the refrigerator. "It's hanging there."

Rex searched the papers plastered all over the door, found it and peered at it carefully. Then he started laughing, all concern evaporated.

And I got the riding lessons.

TOYING WITH ME: HORSE IN THE ROAD

Rex called me one evening when he was out driving after dark. He was returning from a ski club meeting, or some such nonsense which allowed him to go to a restaurant and eat chicken wings and fries instead of fish and salad at home.

"Would you like a horse?" he asked me when I answered the phone.

"Is the Pope Catholic?" I responded, and my heart began racing. I'd been taking riding lessons for several months, after abandoning all things equestrian since my teen years. Those lessons had rekindled my lust for horse ownership. I had a fleeting hope that Rex had turned mind-reader and discovered my deepest desires.

"I think I found one for you," Rex said.

My respiration rate soared, my heartbeat reached

levels I only got from long bouts of cardio exercise, and I broke out in a sweat. And I didn't notice the smile in Rex's voice.

"Where? What kind?" I choked out. Scenarios danced through my head. Perhaps someone at his work is moving and has a horse and is looking for a good home for it. Or he knows someone who has inherited a horse and is looking for a good home for it. Maybe someone has a daughter going to college who wants to keep the horse but have someone ride it while she is away at school...

"There's a horse here, by the side of the road." Rex started laughing. "Get a rope and come down to Reservoir Drive. I think he got out of his barn and he's eating grass in the ditch. I pulled over and stopped to warn any other drivers who come by. Maybe you can catch him and bring him home."

All the fantasies I'd been building at light-speed shriveled up, just as quickly.

"You are mean," I said. I was not laughing, or even smiling.

"I was just trying to have fun with you," Rex said, still unwisely chuckling. "There are two people coming out now to get him. I guess you're too late."

"This is not funny. You are toying with my emotions," I said. I was still not laughing.

Now Rex wasn't laughing, either.

"You know how much I miss Sam," I continued, mentioning the horse I'd had when I was growing up in the Midwest.

"Uh-oh," said Rex. "I may be in trouble."

"I'm going to the barn," I said, "to drown my disappointment by feeding carrots to Schooner."

"I am in trouble, huh?"

"Yes. But Schooner is in luck," I said. "He likes carrots."

Rex is a smart man. He stopped by the grocery store and bought a five-pound bag of carrots before he arrived home. Much, much later he told me that it's a relief to have a wife who likes carrots for horses better than carats of diamonds. (Author's note: I'll give you all a moment to groan, which is better than what a young friend threatened when he first read this - he thinks punsters should be subject to corporal punishment of the highest degree. But in my defense, it is Rex's pun and not mine.)

Much, much later, I told him that this was what started me thinking about a horse of my own. So I guess in the end, the joke was on him.

LOVE

If you have never loved a horse and never been loved by a horse, you have no idea what real love is.   – Unnamed thirteen-year-old girl

BIG: HIGH SPIRITS

Big Rig, so named because he resembles a tractor trailer, is a strong, bull of a gelding advertised as an "American Warmblood" but undoubtedly of more dubious parentage. A melting pot of parts and breeding, Big's massive hindquarters are dwarfed only by his even more massive shoulders. His handsome head crowns a thick yet arched neck, and his soft eye belies a slightly mischievous nature. His riders are often glad that he's inherently lazy.

Big took residence at the barn where I rode just before I began looking for a horse to lease. His owner, newly a mom, wanted him to get more exercise and thought the lesson program at Flying Horse Farm would be perfect for him. Everyone wanted to ride Big, the new lesson horse, except me. I knew in a matter of weeks everyone would have tried him and the excitement of Big's size and newness would have worn off.

I was right. Eventually it was time for me to ride Big in a lesson. Shortly thereafter, he became my regular equine companion. My girlfriend The Perfect Ten, also an equestrian, was delighted. She suggested I enjoy riding such a massive steed and indulge myself in a whole (small) box of chocolates. I had been denying my gluttonous tendencies since dropping seventy pounds a few years before, having wanted to make it easier to clamber onto a horse after rediscovering my passion for all things equine. And I wanted to make it easier on the horse, too.

I lingered by the candy aisle while grocery shopping, thinking about my friend's suggestion... but in consideration of my (quite tight) riding breeches, I decided that would be a bad idea.

Big and I developed an understanding. Eventually. Big liked to bounce off his front end, then his back end - sort of like a miniature buck-rear-buck-rear. It looked impressive from the ground, but the rider, at the pivot point of his movement, barely moved. If Big had been younger and more athletically inclined, he'd have been fearsome indeed. But he wasn't. So I enjoyed looking, to the uninitiated, like I was riding through a series of violent misdeeds and coming out the master.

Of course, Charleigh was unimpressed. After one such session of Big's high spirits (possibly spelled "D-I-S-O-B-E-D-I-E-N-C-E") which happened to occur when Charleigh was in the ring, I looked over to her and grinned smugly. I was pretty proud of myself.

Charleigh, riding her show mare Lady Luck and extending an already brisk trot, never missed a beat. Without even looking in my direction, she stated baldly "You know, you've ridden through that before on smaller horses and never even noticed they did it."

Ego deflated, I concentrated on the rhythm of Big's trot.

Much more satisfying was Sharon's reaction. Sharon, another adult amateur rider at Flying Horse, had been widely proclaiming her interest in Big, and talking of showing him. Since every schooling show I'd ever been in with Sharon resulted in her taking all blue ribbons and me coming in, at best, second to her, I believed her. She hadn't yet ridden Big.

One day, Sharon came in while I was riding Big. He was feeling frisky. It was a slow-motion kind of frisky, but his high spirits (this time very definitely spelled "D-I-S-O-B-E-D-I-E-N-C-E") were in evidence. Sharon stood by the door to the ring and commented to me as I rode, telling me how she was looking forward to riding Big in an upcoming show, and hoped to have a lesson on him later that week. I responded tersely; I was busy arguing with Big. Then Big decided to express himself and bounced a bit - front end, back end, front end, back end. I barely noticed, sitting at the pivot point of his movement as I was, but 1600 pounds of bouncing apparently made an impression on Sharon. Her beautiful big eyes got even bigger, and she stopped talking. I pushed Big through his misbehavior, riding him forward as Charleigh had taught me, and as we trotted past Sharon I smiled. Slightly smugly. Her jaw had dropped slightly and her eyes, still huge, looked a bit glazed.

I never heard any more plans for showing Big from her. Sharon never so much as sat on him. And I basked in unwarranted admiration.

I'm ashamed that I never came clean to her about how easy it was to ride Big through those impressive-looking antics. Sharon, if you ever read this, I am now totally busted... you could have ridden him, easily. And taken all the blue ribbons, as usual.

TV FANTASY HORSES

My childhood television watching centered on figuring out which shows featured horses. *The Lone Ranger* was good, because there were horses. Anything with Roy Rogers was good: horses. The Western about the gambler offered a hope of horses, but no regularly appearing equine star. *Mr. Ed*, *My Friend Flicka*, *Fury* - all good. My expectations of a trusty steed were, unfortunately, warped by Hollywood's romanticism.

My first horse, Sam, lowered my teen-aged expectations somewhat. He came when he saw me, and sometimes even trotted. When my girlfriend and I camped out in the horse pasture (it was many, many acres large and quite beautiful, not like the often-muddy paddocks of the more crowded East), Sam stood near our feet, dozing, seeming to prefer our company to that of the small herd of horses that occupied the pasture with him (looking back, maybe he knew we were more likely to feed him carrots…).

I thought that was normal. After all, at fourteen years of age, I wasn't a kid anymore and I knew that *Fury* was fictional.

And then I went to college and moved from the Midwest, leaving Sam behind with another bright-eyed thirteen-year-old girl who loved him.

Thirty-five years later, I walked into a barn, smelled horses, and wondered how I'd lived so long without an equine in my life.

So I ended up with weekly lessons, and eventually a half-lease on a large, stoic gelding - a Sherman Tank with a sweet face - named Big Rig. Few others wanted to ride him because of his massive size and somewhat intimidating strength, untempered by an excess of manners. At 1600 pounds, if Big wanted a longer rein, he was likely to get it.

But we had an understanding. I'd ridden him enough, and in enough lessons, to recognize the signs that he was planning an impolite act (like pulling the reins out of my hands, or attempting a lethargic buck). I learned to handle the reins and my seat to drive him forward and help him forget his fleeting thoughts of misbehavior, and I also learned that his half-hearted hops were much more impressive from the ground than from the saddle. In fact, Big's shenanigans gave me an undeserved reputation as a fearless and fabulous rider. His size magnified the impressiveness of his misbehavior, but he was easier to stay on then the energetic little Arabian hoodlum I had ridden in lessons before finding this half-lease.

As I said, Big and I had an understanding. He didn't avoid being ridden, and seemed to appreciate the carrots and the grooming, and even the adventures of riding around the property and not just in the ring. Big noticed when I opened the gate to his paddock, and sometimes ambled toward me, but often just looked at me with indifference. One day, after walking to the end of the paddock to get him while he watched, I decided to instruct Big.

"You need to watch old television programs," I told Big while we walked up the hill toward the paddock gate. "Like the one about Fury. Fury would rear up and scream, then gallop toward his human. Maybe you could just settle for a sedate canter, but something a little more energetic would be good. I'm not expecting you to grow a long flowing mane and tail or dye yourself an elegant coal-black, either. I'm just looking for you to put forth a little effort here. Maybe I'll look into a cable hook-up in your stall. So you could learn proper fantasy-horse behavior. There'd be carrots in it for you."

Of course I didn't hook up cable in Big's stall, but two days later I went to ride again. Big was in the paddock, the largest one, and I spotted him at the bottom of the hill.

"Big!" I called to him. "Remember Fury!"

Now Big is the size of a tractor-trailer truck, hence his name, and takes at least as long to get into gear and move, particularly up a hill. He's not afraid of much, and is a magnificent trail horse, but not a horse to dance lightly into a dressage test or leap deer-like over fences. I wasn't really expecting rearing and plunging and frolicking. So when Big looked up, tossed his head, nickered and jogged slowly toward me, I stopped to watch, stunned. It was close enough: Big's interpretation of the fiery black Fury.

I wonder where he watched the TV reruns… or, for that matter, where he learned English.

PONYTAIL BOB GOT HIS MARBLES

Barns have a variety of boarders, and students, and employees. Some of them are colorful characters.

Like Ponytail Bob.

Bob decided to get a horse after his divorce and before he got his second wife. He wanted a fancy-looking horse. Bob, a man of simple tastes (big dogs, pickup trucks, and women of all shapes and sizes), thought a paint would be good. Or a palomino. He didn't care too much about size, or about age, but he didn't want a brown horse. He wanted one that would be easy to recognize. Flashy, in fact.

So Bob went to visit a friend of his, who owned the store where Bob bought his hats and cowboy boots. This friend also brokered ranch horses. Not all horses that work on a ranch stay working on a ranch, and some of the ones that didn't found their way to Lenny's pasture, where he sold them to Western riders who often were delighted to acquire a well-trained, hopefully calm and usually sturdy (if not always flashy – or even very attractive) Quarterhorse.

Bob told Lenny he wanted a paint. Or a pinto, he gets them confused. ("Paint" is a breed. "Pinto" is any of several types of coloring. Both have colorful coats with patches of white and a solid color.)

Bob also told Lenny that a palomino would be good, too, or maybe a buckskin. Lenny looked at Bob. Lenny is an old cowboy, and when he looks at you in a certain way, it's easy to feel like a bull calf whose future career is being determined. Lenny has a pretty hard-boiled stare. I'd been on the receiving end when I ignorantly went shopping at his Western-themed store for something that only Dressage riders use and Lenny, of course, doesn't carry. I did not repeat that mistake.

Anyway, Bob went to look at Lenny's stock. They stood outside a small pasture. Lenny showed Bob a nice, well-trained ten year old sorrel gelding that he'd hitched to a rail outside the pasture. The gelding dozed in the sun, head down, eyes peacefully closed.

"No," said Bob. "That horse is brown." Lenny nodded and chewed on a stalk of grass. He slowly moved back into the field and picked out another gelding, this one a reddish bay with a small blaze. He led the horse out and hitched him beside the drowsy sorrel.

"Lenny," said Bob. "That horse is brown, too." Lenny nodded slowly and looked at Bob with The Stare. A bull calf would have been quaking. Bob didn't notice.

"Brown," said Lenny. "These two horses are well-broke. They're safe, and sane. You can get on them and go trail riding tomorrow." Lenny paused. Bob just stared, but not intimidatingly. Lenny continued, faltering a bit. "I guess I can look for one like these with color… "

Bob interrupted. "I like that one," he said, and pointed at a massive golden palomino.

"That horse is four years old," said Lenny.

"But he's real cute," said Bob.

"He's not very well-trained yet," said Lenny.

"Can he be ridden?" said Bob. "He's real flashy. I like him."

"He's rideable," said Lenny. "But you'll like riding one of these other two better."

"No I won't," said Bob. "Because they're brown."

Bob bought the palomino and named him Marbles, because his grown children wanted him to take up a safer hobby than horses, and one had suggested playing marbles. Bob, in a fit of generosity, named the horse after the game his daughter had recommended, and decided they'd all be happy. They weren't, but they did laugh.

Marbles dropped Bob regularly throughout their first

year together. Every time Bob visited Lenny, Lenny would ask him how the palomino was working out. Bob would tell him about his falls. Lenny always sighed and repeated "I had two well-broke, quiet ranch horses, but they were brown and <u>you</u> had to have color."

Bob just chuckled, because Lenny was right.

About a year after Bob got Marbles, Bob went to Lenny's store to pick up wormer and a new halter. Lenny gave him a bottle of liniment. For Bob.

"Happy anniversary," said Lenny, with his gimlet eyed stare. "For when you fall off."

QUESTION'S FAVORITE HUMAN

I have heard - and read - a lot about unconditional love from animals. Many professional equestrians suggest that a horse's love is all about unconditional acceptance of treats. Occasionally, however, I see a horse who does seem to love a particular human, and I often see horses show very distinct preferences.

One aged Morgan show horse, long retired, attracted attention at the barn for his gentle demeanor and still-fabulous looks. He shone a bright copper like a newly minted penny. An unusual white blaze curved around his forehead and stretched down his face like the punctuation mark that became his nickname. Question pranced on legs stiff with years when he was led out of his stall for a lazy afternoon in the sun, always showing off for any judges that happened to be watching.

A barn friend, Shelly, suggested I was anthropomorphizing when I insisted to her that horses want their own human, and remembered their favorite people. Instead of quarrelling, I told her to meet me by

Question's small, grassy paddock when she was done putting her saddle away. I'd already seen him express his preferences, so I was pretty confident that Shelly would be as surprised – and convinced - as I had been.

I'd been visiting Question with horse cookies and scratches for months. I liked him. The curve of his withers into his barrel and over his loin, the way he cocked his head, the spring in his step when he was led outside, all fascinated me. And I loved how much he obviously loved his human Charleigh, the owner and trainer at the barn, who had shown Question until his retirement at age twenty. Shelly was going to get a demonstration. I was going to school her ignorant little unbelieving self!

Breaking up a couple of carrots and shoving them into my pocket, I rushed out to Question so we'd have a few moments together before Shelly came out. He came over to me as I stood by the fence, and I moved so that he would have a good view of where I knew Charleigh, his owner, would pass by within the next ten minutes.

No treats, just scratches, and Question was attentive and resting his muzzle lightly on my arm. Within a minute, he'd half-closed his eyes, enjoying my ministrations. I'd learned where he liked to be scratched.

Shelly came out of the barn and over to us. Question looked up, alerted by her footsteps. I stopped scratching him and he turned to her.

"Hi, Quest," Shelly said. He turned back to me and touched his muzzle against my arm. I passed her a couple of carrot pieces behind my back. She offered them to him, and he graciously accepted, then returned to me. Shelly rubbed his neck. He looked at her, and returned, once again, to me. I raised an eyebrow at her, and she shrugged, unconvinced.

Then Charleigh walked by. She spoke to one of the stable hands. Question heard her voice, perked up and moved to be closer to where she passed. Charleigh paused and rubbed between his ears.

"How ya doing, fella?" she asked him, and he nudged her hand. "You enjoy the sunshine, OK, Big Guy?" Charleigh continued on, waving to Shelly and me. Question stood by the fence and watched her leave.

Shelly bowed to me. "I stand corrected," she admitted.

I smiled at her, graciously NOT saying "I told you so."

SKI LIFTS AND SPORTS BRAS

Rex likes to ski. A lot. As a good wife, I go with him. I like to ski, too, but without adding "a lot" to it. For me, "a lot" gets added to "I like horses." So when I suffered a skiing injury that curtailed my riding, I was beyond upset. It all began...

At the end of March, with the ski season ending soon, the snow was supposed to be Spring-soft. Yesterday's Spring-soft snow froze into icy ruts that had been groomed into what was optimistically called "packed powder." In New England, "packed powder" can be blue and transparent. In the American South, people make New England "packed powder" in freezers and put it in lemonade on hot days.

I shuffled into the line for the single chair, the only way to get to the top of the mountain. Each skier rode solo on the vintage-style but modernized lift, the last single chair ski lift in North America. I got on the lift and let the skis ride a bit on the - er - "packed powder" as I settled my tush into the lift chair. I caught a rut with the edge of one ski and it popped off. At least my bindings worked, I thought, mentally shrugging. I figured someone in a chair or two would be handed my ski and I'd get it at the top, the lift attendant at the top would (of course!) stop the lift so I could clamber awkwardly off the chair and out of the way, and I'd be embarrassed. Embarrassment happens regularly to me on a ski slope. Nothing to fret about.

Unfortunately, the lift attendant didn't stop the lift. Or even slow it down. What was he DOING in his little hut? Drugs, porn, beer? What he obviously hadn't been doing was paying attention. I optimistically assumed a way-too-high opinion of my abilities and tried to ski off the lift, to the right, with only a left ski. If I'd been thinking realistically, I'd have stayed on the lift and triggered the emergency stop lever just past the unloading area. But I wasn't thinking realistically. I was thinking like... well, like the lift attendant.

Not accomplished enough as a skier to defy the laws of physics, I lost my balance and put down my ski-less right boot. Newton discovered laws about actions and reactions and moving objects tending to stay moving, and I rediscovered some of those laws, landing like a lawn dart on my (luckily helmeted) head and (sadly unprotected) left shoulder.

The lift kept moving as the lift attendant emerged from his little hut. "Dude!" he said.

The next chair was almost to the unload point, and I looked up, caught a glimpse of a panicky face above a pair of arms clutching my lost ski, and flung myself out of his path. The lift attendant watched, slack-jawed, as I flopped at his feet.

"Dude!" he repeated.

Rex, who'd ridden the chair ahead of me, helped me up. My left arm didn't work very well, but nothing hurt, so I smiled thanks to the skier who'd brought my ski, put it on, adjusted my poles, and nodded to the lift attendant.

"Dude," I said to him. He smiled in relief and shuffled back into his hut.

I reassured Rex and said I'd probably go ice my shoulder in the lodge after this run. He decided to make a few more runs before something bad happened to the snow conditions on the mountain, like everything turned into icy ruts or something. His optimism on a ski slope can be a bit unnerving.

My awkward skiing down that run was even worse than usual, and the others at the lodge convinced me to visit the ski patrol, who convinced me to go to the orthopedic clinic a few miles down the road. I rounded up a volunteer to drive me, as Rex was taking those extra ski runs and I wasn't so sure about my driving ability. Ken just dropped me off and continued on his way home. His definition of "bad snow conditions" differs from Rex's, and had already been reached, surpassed, and left in the dust... er ...ice.

I ambled into the clinic. They saw me quickly. Most of the people had already damaged themselves, come in and gotten their x-rays, and were back out of the clinic and headed to the bar. After all, it had been icy all day.

A happy young male nurse called me into a curtained alcove, where a very handsome and very, very young man tried to convince me he was a doctor. Then he admitted he was a resident. I was waiting for him to admit, finally, that he was really the quarterback on the high school football team and he was looking forward to being a senior next year. But he stopped at the "resident doing his orthopedic study time." Since there were a lot of staff people around, or at least people wearing those little pajama-style uniforms that used to come in green only but now sometimes have kitties and trains and stuff on them, I decided to trust him.

Then he asked me if I was wearing a sports bra.

"Why?" I asked, squinting at him suspiciously. This was obviously a prank of some sort. I knew there was some reality television program where people got pulled into some sort of embarrassing situation and ended up looking like utter fools while the camera recorded everything. I was not going to give anyone the satisfaction of making me look like an idiot on film.

"Um," he said. I must have looked like his mother. Or his grandmother.

"Why?" I repeated. I suddenly realized he may have misconstrued the squint and thought I was flirting with him. After all, he was barely out of Middle School and probably not all that good at reading squints from women with naturally grey hair.

"I was going to ask you to take off your shirt so I could look at your shoulder," he confessed.

Oh, boy. I was going to have to wiggle a turtleneck sweater off over an arm and shoulder that didn't work.

"Why would I have to wear a sports bra for that?" I asked, genuinely confused.

"They offer more coverage," the poor young resident/intern/high school quarterback imposter squeaked out.

He was a passable looking young man. I was pretty sure he'd be able to find a date for his senior prom next year. I was also pretty sure that my Lift Those Babies Up and Keep 'Em There Bra was at least as modest as the average sports bra. No lace, no satin, just serious hoisting equipment.

"I'm not wearing a sports bra," I told him. "But I bet you've seen a bra or two in your time, haven't you?" (Ah, maturity has made me wicked!)

He gulped, blushed prettily and nodded his head.

"Then this will probably not come as a big shock," I stated, and started trying to wriggle my turtleneck off without moving my left arm and screaming.

He helped. I think he was trying to show me there were no hard feelings for my embarrassing comments.

After looking briefly and touching even more briefly (I tried to bite him, and not in a nice way), the young almost-doctor called over someone with grey hair, who, obviously, would know more about hurt arms. They conferred for a few minutes, then sent me for an x-ray. They looked at the x-ray, conferred again, and the grey-haired man with a stethoscope broke the bad news: I now literally had a chip on my shoulder. My left arm was broken at the top, a piece sheared off like it had been knocked off with a hammer.

No big deal.

Until he responded to my query about horseback riding by banning it for six to eight weeks. No riding! In fact, stay away from horses altogether! They could bump me and injure me further and I'd need surgery! I burst into tears, inconsolable, and cried until they found Rex, separated him from the mountain, and he came to get me.

I still wonder if it was some sort of karmic punishment for teasing that poor young resident/intern/high school quarterback...

SCHOONER HAS A BALL

Schooner is a Morgan gelding with a focus problem. Charleigh, the barn owner, trainer and lead instructor, likes to compare riding and guiding the horse with the legs, reins and seat to moving a horse down a hallway and closing the doors on the way so the horse goes straight.

Riding Schooner is like moving down that hallway with windows open in the rooms behind the doors. And there's a big storm coming in. A typhoon. And the doors don't latch. And they swing in each direction.

Schooner's just that way. He offers things, like a canter, or a halt, or a turn, or a bend. He has ideas, and he's cheerfully enthusiastic about them. He doesn't hold it against the rider if his ideas aren't accepted, he just keeps offering them. This is not a horse for giving Grandma a quiet trail ride. He's a lot of work.

I met Schooner when I was assigned him for a lesson. It was awful. My first ride on any horse is usually pretty ugly, and this one was no exception. Schooner was slated for another lesson about a half hour after mine. It was a warm day. He'd sweated, a little, and I thought maybe he'd be thirsty. After I cooled him out by walking, he was to wait in the cross-ties, with his saddle loosened, until his next lesson. I decided to offer him water. I didn't ask anyone, I just decided to do this (by the way, I don't recommend doing this, and I hope Charleigh never discovers that I used a feed bucket to give him water).

I know enough to give a horse a small amount of water, not very cold, if they've been working, and I'm pretty careful about it. There were nice little white buckets in the feed room, which is near the bathroom which has running water (yay!) and so I grabbed one, put about three-quarters of a gallon of tepid water in the bucket, and held it under Schooner's nose.

He sniffed the water, then turned to look at me. He really <u>looked</u> at me. It was kind of weird. Then he plunged his nose into the water, drank it down (I was right, he was thirsty) and then began licking my hands as they held the bucket.

That was weird, too.

The next week, when I rode Schooner, he was a different horse. He was even more exuberant about offering me options, but stayed very receptive to what I wanted when I suggested we were not going to circle, or canter, or back-up, just because he knew how and was willing to show me his skills. He was even more challenging to ride than during my last lesson, but much more attentive - and fun. And he began to interact with me when I groomed him. As other students started to tire of his unflagging enthusiasm for contributing his ideas to the ride, I developed a taste for it.

Eventually, I began leasing him. A lot of students said they liked him, and said they wanted to ride him, but it gradually whittled down to just me and one or two others.

And then he hurt himself in the paddock. This shouldn't have been a surprise. I'd actually seen him running laps in the large paddock he shared with a couple other horses. It was like an exercise program - Schooner would run in one direction for several laps, always near the fence, and then in the other direction.

Confined to his stall for a month to give the ligament a chance to start mending, Schooner was beyond upset. I rode another horse for that month, but visited Schooner and groomed him. I'd started to feel like he was mine. He greeted me with a raucous whinny, and was as happy to see me as a Golden Retriever puppy.

I began teaching him tricks. An enthusiastic pupil, he began offering me more than I'd requested. We quickly moved beyond touching things with his nose and hanging his head, and developed a whole routine, complete with fetching a ball, hugging, and pretending to drink from a soda bottle.

One day Jessie and I stood talking outside Schooner's stall. This was unacceptable, obviously, and Schooner nickered. I ignored him - Jessie and her latest dressage score with Xavier, her breathtaking Selle Francais gelding, had priority. Schooner disagreed. He started kicking his stall door. That is unacceptable, so I scolded him and turned back to Jessie.

A moment later, a strange rattling noise came from behind me, and Jessie burst out laughing. I turned, and Schooner was holding his red ball and banging it against his stall bars to get my attention. As I joined Jessie in laughing, we agreed to continue our discussion after Schooner ran through his repertoire of tricks, practiced a new one, and got a good brushing.

When I was at last able to start riding Schooner, for five minutes each day, at a walk, I went back to leasing him exclusively. Charleigh offered me another horse for a weekly lesson, but I insisted that was wrong. I told her that I felt guilty because I was riding Schooner EVERY DAY and I only had a half-lease on him, so I was only paying for three rides per week. I asked her if I owed her more because I was riding every day.

"It's OK," Charleigh said.

I offered to help her clean stalls, or feed, or do other chores, because I was riding so often.

Charleigh tried not to choke. I didn't know what was wrong with her. I thought maybe some of her ever-present coffee had gone down the wrong way.

"It's OK," she assured me.

When Schooner and I were up to ten minutes of walking each day, I asked Charleigh if I could ride him bareback. It seemed a lot of effort to saddle him and then clean the saddle and wash the saddle pad for only ten minutes of use, even if I didn't clean everything every day. And I liked to ride bareback. And there was a teen-ager at the barn who rode bareback sometimes.

"Yes, you can," she said.

"Is it still tack-walking?" I asked.

"Yes," Charleigh said, and choked again.

"Why is it called 'tack-walking' if the only tack I am using is a bridle?" I asked.

"Because it is," Charleigh responded, after she recovered. .

"Would it still be tack-walking if I went bareback and bridleless?"

"No, on Schooner it would be called 'suicide.'" Charleigh gave me the look that makes me feel like I'm twenty years younger than she is, instead of twenty years older. It also reminds me that SHE has control of the horses and I shouldn't give her too much trouble.

Later Jessie told me that tack-walking is not a privilege, but a chore. People dread tack-walking. It's not fun, and sometimes horses act up and misbehave out of excess energy.

I'm glad Jessie didn't tell me that until I'd done it for a while. And I'm glad Charleigh didn't laugh in my face. I thought she just choked on her coffee a lot.

Schooner got better, and, by the time we were trotting every day for twenty minutes, Charleigh was pointing to us to show beginner lesson students how to post a trot and how to change diagonals.

And Schooner could do a lot of tricks, too.

CREATIVE USE OF A TACK TRUNK

Horses teach a lot of life lessons about disappointment. They go lame, they spook under saddle, they grow old and die, they refuse a jump, they nip and they kick. Barns also offer a lot of opportunity to hide from disappointments.

Thankfully.

There are haylofts, and empty stalls, and pastures, and corners of paddocks tucked away where we can hide until we realize the heartbreak follows us wherever we go. But, searching for that spot to hide can distract us for a little while.

And no one needs distracting like a disappointed thirteen-year-old girl.

Madison was one such thirteen-year-old girl. Her parents decided she should have her own horse. This should be a source of overwhelming joy. They encouraged her to find her dream equine companion, and they would willingly open their pocketbooks. Madison was the envy of the other thirteen-year-olds at the barn (and some of us adults, too!).

But tragedy haunted Madison. She wanted a palomino, no compromising. Plus she found commitment difficult. Finally, Madison reluctantly agreed to a handsome palomino gelding. Dr. Brett, our friendly and almost frighteningly thorough lameness veterinarian, was called in to thoroughly check over Golden Boy.

Dr. Brett found more irregularities in the horse than there are in the average veterinary textbook. He was fine for certain jobs, like learning simple tricks and eating carrots. Carrying even the young and petite Madison in dressage shows, over an occasional series of jumps and on trail rides would be beyond his physical capability. Madison suddenly found that she was hopelessly devoted to the handsome Golden Boy, and wanted him desperately. She locked herself in her room for three days, crying and texting her friends. Her parents actually considered buying Golden Boy anyway, and trying to find a series of specialists to make him fit what Madison wanted. Our trainer Charleigh, who was overseeing this purchase, nixed the idea.

Even I knew it would be easier to make me a prima ballerina, and I'm a woman of mature years with a body designed by Hostess cupcakes and the flexibility of a coat hanger. A wooden coat hanger.

Madison finally emerged from her room and was coaxed into horse shopping again.

After several more trips to visit horses, including three pilgrimages to look at a palomino mare, Madison agreed that the palomino mare, Sunshine, would be a suitable companion. But scheduling the pre-purchase veterinary checkup was almost impossible; Sunshine's owners were gone, or unavailable, or inconvenienced. Then, when the vet changed his schedule to fit theirs, the horse had been sold elsewhere.

Madison was inconsolable. A petite child, she found the perfect hiding place: a good-sized tack trunk that was mostly empty. It took her frantic parents and two less-panicky adults to find her. She eventually emerged and found a suitable and sound palomino gelding frivolously named Beach Bum (and unfortunately called "Bum" as a barn name). Their story has a happy ending, with Bum waiting for Madison every day and nickering to her, and Madison feeding him carrots and teaching him tricks as well as riding him over the occasional fence, on the occasional trail, and to the occasional show. Together, they're winning ribbons at local competitions and they've each learned to smile whenever they're together.

But to this day, I'm a little bit jealous of Madison's hiding place… it's just too cramped for me.

IN MEMORIAM: SCHOONER

They say mature love is sweeter. I know that I appreciated the mature equine love of my equestrian life more than my teenage crushes. Not because he was a better horse, or we did more, but because I'd known others and understood, at last, that horses do indeed prefer certain humans.

I learned this from a mature show horse, long retired due to ligament failure. Question, named after a unique marking on his handsome face, remained flashy and elegant in spite of teeth lengthened by age and a coat shaggy from a hormone imbalance common in older horses. Question taught me, with emphasis, that horses have favorite humans and are extremely capable of showing their preferences.

Question had presence, even long after his show career had ended. I'd visit him, with a carrot or a rub, and admire the proud arch of his neck and the achingly beautiful curve of his shoulder. He treated me with favor, nudging me gently and even nickering breathily.

One day I was rubbing the spot behind his ears that always seemed to be itchy when Lynn arrived at the barn. We were planning to ride together, and she knew to stop by Question's stall if she didn't see me in the main area. When Lynn arrived, Question turned his regal head slightly, then, recognizing her, turned back to me.

"You've been dismissed," I laughed to Lynn. She laughed, too. We talked a bit while I continued to scratch Question's itchy spots and he continued to ignore Lynn. Then Charleigh, the barn owner and trainer, approached. She was talking on her cell phone. Question was Charleigh's first show horse. They'd entered many a show and won many a ribbon.

Question heard her voice. His head rose, his neck arched, and he turned away from me, mid-rub.

"I've been dismissed, now," I told Lynn, who agreed that the hierarchy of Question's heart had been clearly demonstrated.

But I held top position with another Morgan, Schooner. Schooner sported a blaze that wandered crookedly over his cute face, oddly patchy brown coloring, and legs of questionable conformation. But his small, well-formed ears pricked when he heard my voice and he always came to me. Whether he was in the far corner of his field or the back of his stall, my greeting brought him as close to me as the gates and doors would allow. He called for me if I dallied. Schooner had the attention span of a toddler and the happy disposition of a Golden Retriever.

And he taught me when to let go.

I began riding Schooner because his happy and unfocused attitude frustrated more serious equestrians. In competitions, Schooner had a history of embarrassing his rider. In one notable incident, he began peeing in the middle of a class, totally ignoring other horses cantering by, his mortified rider huddling on his back and trying to disappear into the saddle. But I didn't worry about competitions, I just wanted to ride. Schooner's lack of focus kept me paying attention, and his good nature allowed me to learn. Not that he concerned himself overmuch with making sure I stayed on his back; more than once he released a bit of excess energy in an exuberant fashion that resulted in my unplanned - and ungraceful - "dismount."

But he preferred me to all other humans. Lynn insisted that I wore a label, visible to other horses, claiming I was Schooner's Human. And that was fine with me.

One day, Schooner frolicked a bit too enthusiastically in his paddock and pulled a ligament. With months of careful rehabilitation, special shoes, and various treatments, he became once again able to be ridden. A few months later, he repeated the performance, and I again worked to rehabilitate him. The third time, he didn't come back. His mismatched legs strained his ligaments and tendons and he only remained sound at the walk. Reluctantly, we retired him and put him out in the pasture every day with another much-loved retiree.

Schooner didn't take to retirement, and had no concept

that he was to confine himself to a sedate walk. He played and pranced in the pasture until he injured himself again.

"This is not a good sign," Charleigh said. Uncharacteristically sympathetic, she put an arm around my shoulders. "His legs are not good, and can't heal right anymore because of the way he's built. They're causing him pain. When he finally notices - and you know it may take a while because he's not the brightest horse in the barn - and he finds he can't move without hurting, he will become more afraid of things until he's stressed about not being able to escape any imagined predator. Then he could colic pretty easily."

I nodded and answered that he was really pretty smart because he had learned the tricks I taught him pretty easily during his long weeks of stall rest. Charleigh sighed, agreed - obviously placating me - and patted my shoulder.

One day when I went to visit Schooner, I knew there was something wrong. He didn't peer out from his stall when he heard my voice, and I didn't see his eye and ear sticking through the bars. No nickers, no kicking. I walked quietly to his stall and found him lying down, ears pricked and watching for me. He'd heard me but hadn't gotten up to greet me. It was a first.

I sat with him in his stall. For almost an hour, he rested his muzzle in my lap and I cried until I understood what people meant when they said there are no tears left. Finally, almost reluctantly and certainly gingerly, Schooner stood up. I took him out of his stall and groomed him. Although we didn't walk far, it was far enough. He had finally noticed the pain.

Charleigh and I talked, and she let me make the hard decision to contact one of the many vets who had worked with Schooner throughout his rehabilitations. We made feeble jokes about getting metal helmets and waiting for a thunderstorm, when we'd hook up Schooner and Chuckles, a physically sound but mentally damaged and difficult to handle horse and exchange their personalities.

When the time came for Schooner's final walk down his favorite trail, I cut up eight apples for him. He liked apples, and he would not colic that day.

He could have been sold to slaughter, as happens to so many horses that are beyond their usefulness, but Charleigh's heart remains bigger than her pocketbook, and Schooner was sent on his way peacefully. I like to think that he'll return, with karmic justice, as a border collie with an above-average ability for doing tricks.

And I bring Charleigh coffee, just the way she likes it. Often. She understood that I needed to learn to say good-bye. She - and Schooner - gave me lessons in more than just riding, and I am grateful.

HORSE SHOWS

Only a horse person would spend hundreds of dollars on a show to win a $2.49 ribbon.

— An imprudent husband

RESERVE CHAMPIONS OF SOMETHING

Charleigh, my trainer and the owner of the barn where I ride, had been giving me lessons for a year and a half since my return to riding at age 50. She decided I was ready to compete in a horse show run by a 4-H club in a nearby town. Some of her adult students were going, and Charleigh had made arrangements for a trailer that carried four horses. Three riders had committed already, leaving room for my horse of choice.

"You can take Wilbur," Charleigh tempted me. She knew he was the first horse at her barn I'd fantasized about stealing and keeping in my garage. He was the horse I always requested when she offered me a choice.

So I agreed.

Charleigh sat down with me and went over the classes on what she called "the prize list." It looked like a list of classes, not prizes, but I didn't ask. I just nodded a lot. I had no idea what she was talking about.

"If you take the Eq and Pleasure Classes," Charleigh started to explain, then noticed my blank expression. "'Eq' means "Equitation" and is a walk/trot/canter class that is judged primarily on the rider, and 'Pleasure' is a similar class that is judged primarily on the horse. In a nutshell. Not a completely precise description, but you just ride your best in both classes. And smile. Wilbur will take good care of you. Everyone will be in the ring together." Charleigh turned back to the paper and twiddled absently with the pen. "And you'll like the trail class." She checked off a box. "You get to ride through and over obstacles - probably not opening a gate," Charleigh smiled. She'd heard me brag about opening gates from on top of Sam, the horse of my teen years. "But you'll have to get a letter out a mailbox and put it back, and that will be sort of like opening a gate." Charleigh read the paper for a moment. "Ah," she continued, and looked up at me.

"If you take the showmanship class, too, you'll be eligible for a championship," she said.

"'Showmanship class'? 'Championship'?" I responded, blankly.

"Showmanship is an in-hand class. You'll show off Wilbur from the ground, and be judged on how well you show him to his best advantage. We'll go over it. And there's a championship awarded based on these four classes. You might as well just enter showmanship, too, and be eligible."

I nodded again. Whatever I did, I'd have a day where I'd dress up like a real equestrian and play with Wilbur. It'd be fun. I already had a show jacket because my mother has a vague idea that one always dresses up to ride, and she likes to shop.

And it was, indeed, fun. With some slight preparation (but not nearly enough), I walked into the showmanship class with Wilbur, spit-polished the evening before and wearing his newly-lustrous bridle. I got caught up in playing with Wilbur's nose while I was waiting for the judges to look at the other horses and failed to notice when they moved over to us, so I was late in stepping aside to showcase Wilbur's many fine attributes. And then I trotted him in a crooked line. The judges were kind when they gave us our last-place ribbon, and explained my errors. It was a small class, so I just decided that I didn't need to tell anyone that third place was also last place. I hung the ribbon from Wilbur's bridle and we strutted back to the trailer.

The Equitation and Pleasure classes were larger. After a brief warm-up, during which Wilbur expressed his displeasure at moving vehicles on the fairground (parked and still, they are okay, but trucks and cars in motion are deeply offensive), we entered the ring and Wilbur became instantly professional. I remember him turning his head to look at me as if to let me know that my job was to stay on and smile, he'd handle the rest.

He was right. A seasoned competitor, Wilbur understood the announcer's "Trot. Everybody trot" and responded before I gave him the cue. I just kept smiling. We made it through the Equitation and Pleasure classes, back to back, and came in about mid-field in both. Then we wandered over to the trail class, set up in a ring on the side, which was taking competitors between other classes. Each horse and rider team ran the course individually, and I had no idea how many entries there were or how anyone else had fared. Which was fine, because I didn't really care.

I gave my name and our show number to the volunteer minding the gate leading into the trail course and studied the diagram so I'd know what to do. Luckily, there were no moving vehicles to be faced. But there was The Mailbox...

The Mailbox is not a scary thing in itself. It just requires that the horse stands for a few moments while you open the box, get out a letter, wave it around to show you have it, put it back in the mailbox and close the little door.

Wilbur believes standing still is for sissies. If he has a rider, unless he's lining up for a ribbon, he shouldn't be standing still for any length of time. There are places to go, there's work to be done, horses are not sofas, and so on.

I decided to take the course one challenge at a time. Wilbur and I entered the ring, then walked between a set of poles. We trotted, weaving through a line of cones. We walked into a box marked out by poles and, with very little input from me, Wilbur spun 360 degrees like an American Quarter Horse Reining Champion in an English saddle and sauntered out the same side. The creepy sounding wooden bridge caused Wilbur to pause for a millisecond and twitch one ear before gamely striding over it to reach the next obstacle.

The Mailbox.

By this time, I wasn't going to let Wilbur's quirks interfere with our partnership. I was grateful. He'd handled everything so far and I was NOT going to fight with him about a little thing like standing still so I could fiddle with a mailbox. I slowed him as we walked by the mailbox and got a momentary pause, during which

I leaned over and flipped the door open. We circled, tightly, and on the second pass I grabbed the letter. Wilbur didn't mind me leaning, or slowing him down, but stopping was definitely out of the question. I waved the letter enthusiastically to make sure the judge saw our success while I guided Wilbur in another tight circle. I tossed the letter into the mailbox as we passed it again, then asked Wilbur to stop and back up. Two steps backwards and I flipped the lid shut as he changed gears and started forward again.

There was nothing in the rules that said we had to stop and stand still through the whole process.

We walked into another "L" maze of poles and backed out, adroitly turning during backing. Then we trotted out the gate. Later I found out we had earned a second place.

I groomed Wilbur by the trailer and fed him carrots. I lugged buckets of water and (unintentionally) smeared grime over my white shirt and my tan breeches. With Wilbur happily rubbed down, watered and munching hay on the trailer, I found my other show buddies gathered around one of the snack trucks. Another adult amateur, Cordelia, had won Western Pleasure at her first show ever, and was buying sodas and coffee for the group while wearing her blue ribbon on her hip.

"And look," Cordelia said, thrusting a coffee into my hand and gesturing at a bright blue tangle hanging from her shoulder. "I got this piece of crap halter, too, as a prize, not just the ribbon. It's junk, look at this rotten hardware, I hate these snaps because Dream always rolls and gets mud jammed into it and they never close right again, but it was free because I won the class and it was my first show and I was just hoping for a ribbon, any ribbon at all, because my family doesn't even know what colors stand for what place…"

I nodded a lot and joined the group from Flying Horse sitting on assorted bales of straw that had been strategically scattered to serve as Rustic Horse Show Benches. We swapped stories about the show for a while. I wasn't sure why we were waiting around: we all had a couple of ribbons and a couple of stories, the horses were all cared for, watered and loaded onto the trailer. But Charleigh remained lounging against a bale of straw and sipping a fruity soda, listening to the stories and adding to them. No one mentioned that Cordelia's "free" halter was really far from free, between the costs of the show and trailering and training fees. It wasn't about the halter. Or the ribbons. It was about the experience, and the stories, and the camaraderie around the snack trucks.

Then the announcer came over the loudspeakers again, promising final results. I pretty much ignored it, because my final results were hanging on the door of the trailer, and I was pretty content with everything except the second place Trail Class ribbon. I was actually pretty amazed by that.

Even when not paying attention, the sound of one's name catches in the ear. How many times does a wisp of another's conversation draw our notice because our name was mentioned?

And if one has a catchy last name, and it's blared over a loudspeaker covering a small fairground…

Wilbur and I had won a Reserve Champion award! Charleigh tried to explain to me what the fancy ribbon meant, but I forgot immediately amid the dazzle of the fancy red and yellow and white satin.

I think it was for adult amateur women of mature years wearing navy hunt coats and riding bay Morgans who totally took care of them.

Thanks, Wilbur!

AMBITION: HOW I WANT TO RIDE

I've seen a lot of riders. There's Jessie and her close partnership with her giant Selle Francais Xavier, Karen and her fearlessness when she was caught in a group runaway situation and rode like a Valkyrie among thundering horses without panicking and without losing her seat, Diana who competed nationally in equitation and jumping, Francisca who brings a Zen-like calm to every ride, Joy with her enthusiasm for anything her mare does, Amber and her show-jumper ambitions whose motto truly is "go big or go home," Charleigh and her ability to ride any horse and make them look like an upper-level superstar - the list is almost endless. And I watch famous riders via internet videos and DVDs purchased with the hope that I'd glean some miraculous tidbit.

But the person I most want to ride like is Sophie. Sophie, the teenager. Sophie, the sometimes shy. Sophie who loves the corgi of the horse world, Choco, with all her heart and began reluctantly looking for a horse of her own when it became apparent that her feet, dangling lower with each ride, would soon get in the way of his when she rode him.

Sophie and I both loved horses that became, over time, less appropriate for us. Sophie's legs were fast becoming longer than Choco's. My leased favorite, Schooner, succumbed to a mismatched pair of front feet that forced him to accommodate throughout his body until a final injury in the paddock proved too much and he had to be retired. But it's not Sophie's soft heart that I admire, we share that already.

It's Sophie's courageous spirit. Or maybe competitive spirit. Or maybe just plain stubbornness.

Sophie and I attended our first dressage show together. She rode Choco, an old hand at shows. I was on my new mare Bea, also a seasoned professional. Choco was feeling frisky. Sophie rode first. Intro Test B. I know that test. But it didn't look familiar to me. In a fit of nerves, Sophie turned Choco the wrong way after entering down the center line and saluting the judge. Choco must have realized her mistake about when she did. Sophie corrected, guiding Choco through a 15 meter circle-turned-change-of-direction, another new move for Intro B. Choco then took control and transitioned into a lovely, controlled (but not by Sophie) canter. Another move not on Intro Test B. Choco cantered leisurely past the judges, Sophie looking calm enough that I thought I was mistaken about which test she was riding. Then Choco continued his rhythmic canter, very relaxed (the first two building blocks on the Dressage Pyramid!) and tucked his front feet tidily as he took the short fence delineating the ring in perfect form, Sophie neatly perched in a perfect jump seat on his back.

Such aplomb!

Choco brought Sophie to where Bea and I were waiting for our turn, with our trainer Charleigh. Sophie's parents, standing nearby, innocently applauded Sophie's nice jump. Sophie glared at them (and later told them not to come to her shows any more, or at least stay far away from her – a true teenager, she had been more embarrassed by their ignorance of dressage than by Choco's misbehavior). Charleigh encouraged Sophie, the dressage judge invited her to ride the test again, although she was disqualified, and promised to score the test even though it would not be official.

Sophie did. She didn't cry, complain, or whine. She neither beat nor blamed Choco. Sophie just went back into the ring and rode the test.

She scored pretty well, too. Unofficially.

That graceful rise into jump position when the jump became inevitable is my new ambition. Or, at least the spirit behind it is!

AGING GRACEFULLY

In a pleasure barn, age doesn't matter so much. At first, looking at a woman who sports gray-streaked hair and has wrinkles makes young people think they won't have anything in common.

Ha! It's a barn. We have a lot in common.

We're all used to being coached, corrected, and generally bossed around by Charleigh, the trainer and barn owner. We go on trail rides together. We clean tack together. We go to shows together. We compete against each other in schooling shows at Flying Horse, and sometimes at shows outside our barn.

Sometimes that causes problems.

Like the time I was riding my new mare, Bea, in a schooling show in our barn. Bea and I had to ride with a thirteen-year-old hot shot named Amber. Amber beat us in every class. She'd been riding for a while and had a natural aptitude as well. I asked that Amber be forced to ride a different horse instead of her experienced, unflappable and highly professional Arabian. I whined, I complained, I was ignored, and I came in second. At best.

Then one day, we had a schooling show with just games at our barn. There were trail classes, and Sit-A-Buck, and relays, and a timed race trotting over poles. I rode an elderly school horse, Romeo, as Bea had just had a chiropractic treatment and wasn't working for a couple of days. Romeo was available because the games were all based on speed, and he just didn't have it.

I entered the trot poles class, even though I knew that Romeo's idea of a trot was a sort of two-beat amble. But I had a secret weapon: sneakiness. It comes with age.

The course was set up with a pole in the middle of each of the four sides, set at a 90-degree angle to the wall. We were to trot around the ring, over each pole, and the fastest time would win. I took a lot of teasing because I was riding Romeo.

"We'll go last," I said. "Romeo could use some time to rest up before we blast around the ring." This was met with muffled (and impolite) giggles, including from Amber, who actually snorted when she tried to politely stifle her laughter.

Romeo and I waited for our turn and watched each of the younger hot shots trot animatedly around the ring, over the trot poles, staying next to the wall as though riding in a lesson. The times were good.

But not good enough.

When it was Romeo's and my turn, we went at his usual trot speed: very, very slowly. But we cut the corners, turning our path into a diamond shape, only nearing the rail at the points where we had to go over the trot poles. And we came up with the best time, by far.

So Amber came in second, and I behaved in an

entirely professional, totally proper and perfectly mature manner.

"Nyah, nyah," I said to Amber, waving the blue ribbon. "Old age and treachery CAN overcome youth and skill." She had the grace to laugh.

The next time Charleigh had games in a horse show, she put traffic cones in the corners so we couldn't cut them.

But Romeo and I had had our day!

COMPETITIVE BY NATURE

The Barn Chicklettes (the girls who have not yet reached legal drinking age who hang around the barn, as opposed to us Barn Chicks, who have left our dewy youth in the dust) have, among them, a few who are, simply put, quite competitive. And there are only a limited number of blue ribbons at any given horse show.

Many of us have moved into showing dressage, because it is, at lower levels at least, relatively easy on older joints (whether said joints belong to the horse or the rider). Also, although there are ribbons given at dressage shows, dressage tests are scored individually and so we can compete against ourselves, from one show to another. This eases some of the competitive urges. Maybe. Sort of.

Or maybe not....

One pair of young Barn Chicklettes, the best of friends, went to a youth dressage show together. A multi-day event designed to encourage young people in the sport of dressage, this event requires not only a great deal of preparation, but a great deal of togetherness. One of these Barn Chicklettes, Amber, tends to form intense but brief partnerships with a series of sleek and accomplished horses. When Amber's ambitions grew beyond her mount's abilities, she happily finds a new home for her partner and moves on. There was never a horse Amber didn't want to ride, and she had the moxie to climb onto any of them. Amber's friend and fellow Barn Chicklette, Sophie, entered the show world on a retired eventing pony, Choco, who was big of heart and short of leg. Sophie loved him, even after their first dressage show when Choco took over and decided to modify the Dressage Intro Test B by adding a canter and a jump, with forelegs neatly tucked, out of the ring. Sophie rose to two-point and took the jump as though she'd asked Choco for it. Without crying or any drama at all, Sophie returned Choco to the ring and re-rode the test at the suggestion of a compassionate judge. Sophie remained disqualified, but the second time she rode the test correctly, received a score for it, and came back with a story to tell.

And then Amber and Sophie went, together, to the annual Youth Dressage Festival sponsored by ex-Olympian Lendon Grey. All their parents and Charleigh, as coach, accompanied them.

Sophie looked up to the fearless, experienced and older (by two months) Amber. They discussed horses, and shows, and jumping, and dressage, and Amber always led the way. Amber had a string of horses behind her, and a bin of ribbons won at various shows for equitation and jumping. Sophie took Amber's advice on all matters.

And then, with multiple opportunities to ride dressage tests at the festival, Sophie scored higher than Amber. On one test. On her faithful Choco. In a fit of exhilaration and poor judgement, Sophie sent the news to all their friends via social media.

And Amber declared war. The weapons were histrionics of all types: pouting, tears and sulking, angry outbursts and wounded sniffling. Hostilities escalated.

Charleigh stepped in. She is a brave woman, but later she admitted it's easier to step into a pen with two horses fighting and calm them than it was to try to calm two teenage girls.

A couple of weeks after they returned from the festival, Amber continued to state her grievances to anyone within earshot. One evening, with both the girls in the viewing room and Charleigh watching from a safe distance, the wise Karen positioned herself in front of them.

"Look," Karen said, in her "you-will-now-listen-to-me" voice "I show my horse, and I know that Charleigh is better than I am. If I ever score higher in a dressage test, or get a better ribbon than Charleigh does - should we ever, for some unfathomable reason, be in the same class, I will be very proud." Karen turned to Amber. "That's how Sophie feels about you, Amber. She's amazed she got a higher score."

"But..." Amber started to interrupt. She'd been explaining her horse was new to her ever since The

Tragedy occurred. Karen was having none of it.

"No, no, it's true," she shushed Amber. "Let me tell you, you're lucky. If I ever beat Charleigh in any way in a horse show, I'm renting a billboard. For a month. And taking out a full-page ad in the New York Times. Everybody, and I mean EVERYBODY, is going to know about that, you can bet on it." Karen continued for a couple of minutes, listing the web sites she'd build and the radio programs she'd contact. Charleigh was laughing. Sophie was laughing. I, privileged to witness The Dressage Peace Accords, was laughing.

Finally, Amber laughed, too, and the war was over.

THE PROFESSIONAL

My Appendix Quarter Horse mare, Bea, is a seasoned performer. She's a better athlete than I am, and a better competitor, and much better trained. I realized this in the middle of a dressage test, and the light bulb went off for me when I understood that, like some of the hunter/jumper riders admit in interviews, I can count on her to cover my mistakes.

Newly partnered, Bea and I went to a dressage show at Mount Holyoke College, which I had attended many years before (<u>very</u> many years before, actually). At the time, I was a student with a heavy debt load, a workload including both a difficult major and a part-time job, and a scholarship requiring that I maintain a minimum grade point average; I had not been involved with the equestrian program. I'd left my first horse behind when I left the Midwest for college, where he happily entertained a new horse-crazy teenager. I thought I had left my equestrian adventures behind - until, many years later and after balancing a career with raising a family, I returned to riding and eventually found Bea.

And now, I was back at Mount Holyoke, with a talented and lovely horse, a talented and very patient trainer, and a yen to compete. Of course, I was more distracted than Bea as we halted to salute the judge.

Coming around a corner at a rising trot, our test called for us to cross on the diagonal. I blanked out ("The flags! The judge! Mount Holyoke College! The footing in this ring is truly divine!"). Bea, however, remained focused and professional.

Bea dropped a shoulder, very slightly. She turned her head, again, very slightly, and bent - again, almost infinitessimally. I was paying just enough attention to pick up on her cues, and signalled to her my agreement. We continued the pattern, correctly in spite of my distraction.

And my light bulb went off. My horse is more professional than I am! And she knows the tests at least as well as I do! She deserves an extra carrot!

The judge didn't comment - perhaps Bea fooled her into thinking I rode that turn. My trainer, Charleigh, was not fooled. I admitted both my mistake, which she had seen, and my revelation, which did not surprise her.

Charleigh knew that Bea was carrying me in more ways than one.

RULES OF A SHOW: HOW TO BREAK THEM

Charleigh, my trainer, suggested I attend a seminar for young dressage riders. Luckily, mature adult amateurs, with checks, were also welcome. I am a mature adult amateur, and I had a check, so I attended.

I learned many things. Mostly about why Charleigh keeps nagging me at shows about the things I do (or don't do). My highly professional, highly trained mare Bea and I go to shows. I go so that I can show everyone what a highly professional and trained horse I ride, while I'm wearing cool clothes (except for the breeches, which very few adult amateurs competing at my level really wear well). Bea goes because I take her and she gets treats. She does a lot of things for me because of treats. (This is true of many humans as well, but horses are much more upfront about it.)

My first recognized dressage show confused me greatly. I didn't understand why it was "recognized."

Charleigh explained that it was licensed by the United States Equestrian Federation and the scores may count toward special awards or recognitions. The other type of show is a "schooling" show, which is used by riders and horses to gain experience.

Then I found out the biggest difference for me: recognized shows have a lot of rules that you have to understand, and they do not appear to be posted anyplace at the show. The horse has to have his or her show number on at all times, even when being hosed off after a sweaty competition. I did not do this when I walked Bea to a lovely patch of grass to give her a few minutes of grazing. My trainer panicked when she saw Bea's naked halter. Charleigh sent the woman who had come along to help with hauling and grooming scurrying to retrieve the number from Bea's bridle, which was hanging by the trailer. Meanwhile, Charleigh lectured me on the rules about number display.

Then there was the time a fellow competitor left the ring on a bolting horse. They returned to their second test, two hours later. The horse was much calmer, and much, much sweatier. The rider wore a grimly determined expression, and the test was completed very nicely and without further incident. There's a rule about leaving the ring without authorization. In both schooling shows and recognized shows.

Another rule addressed the the rider I saw on an extremely naughty but handsome warmblood gelding. The horse gave every appearance of belligerence, and when cued to canter, pulled the reins, dropped a shoulder and slid out from under his rider. He deposited her on the outside of the fence. He remained on the inside. Smirking, I swear. I found out they were disqualified, not because one of them was outside the ring, but because any falling is a disqualification.

Unless it happens before or after the official test. I ran a simple course of trot poles in a small schooling show on an enthusiastic Morgan. He begged to jump the ground poles. I refused to let him. He did anyway. I tried to stop him, and he began to canter. He liked to jump. He continued around the course with great enthusiasm. His jumps became larger, and his canter turned into a hand gallop. After we completed the course, he gave an enthusiastic victory buck that sent my stiff and unbalanced self into the dirt.

Charleigh rushed over to me as someone else caught my gelding.

The first thing she said to me was "You're not disqualified. The course was over before you fell off."

There are some rules I may never really understand. Like how the priority is my ribbon color and not the state of my bruised backside! (By the way, Mr. Enthusiastic and I came in last... and I got back on him, of course!)

ON THE SIDE OF THE ROAD

The horse show was successful, and we'd admired the ribbons and dressage scores before taking turns piling our tack into the backs of the trucks. We loaded the two trailers with three horses and three hay nets, offered water one last time to each competitor (both human and equine) and made one last check of the area where we'd parked for the day to make sure we hadn't left behind any stray tack, apparel or snack wrappers. I rode with Jessie, who was hauling my mare Bea and her own warmblood gelding Xavier. Our trainer Charleigh drove in the other truck with Karen, who'd come along to help and for the fun of hanging out with nervous riders all day and eating snacks. They were hauling Charleigh's slightly green but oh-so-promising mare Lady Luck, who'd won high point at the show and immediately gone into heat. We decided to give Xavier a break by keeping Lady Luck away from him; he was starting to look harassed by her not-so-subtle overtures while he was trying to relax and graze after his own respectable showing. Charleigh laughed that Xavier was going to want a restraining order, so we decided to restrain Lady Luck in solitude.

On the way home, heavy traffic and a brief cloudburst sent a couple of cars into a skid. A vehicle with no right to be anywhere but in a military combat zone withstanding explosives hit Charleigh's truck. The Hummer was scratched, maybe, a little bit. The truck's fender crumpled.

Jessie and I were a few cars back, but saw the disturbance. Then we saw the result. Charleigh had pulled to the side of the road, out of traffic. Later she said that the few yards back to the trailer was the longest walk she'd had in a long time. She heard Lady Luck complaining bitterly, so she knew she was alive, but it still took a stout heart to open the door. Karen followed her, but without her usual cheerful chatter.

The trailer's partition was bent, but Lady Luck seemed unhurt. Just extremely offended.

Jessie and I, seeing the accident, pulled off the highway onto a conveniently located rest area. Charleigh and Karen followed in the damaged truck, just getting it off the highway and out of the way of traffic.

We convened with the state trooper who arrived. Charleigh decided that the trailer wasn't going anywhere else with a horse in it and the trooper wisely agreed (did I mention Charleigh dominates any situation which she feels should be dominated, with little effort, in spite of being maybe 5' 1 1/2" and often mistaken for a teenager?). Xavier and Bea complained because they were standing still and not getting out of the trailer. Lady Luck complained because she heard Xavier and she was, after all, in love. The Hummer driver, a lanky middle-aged woman with peacocks tattooed on both of her arms, traded information with everyone and the trooper filled out forms. Karen and I spent the time offering water to the horses, so we missed a lot of the discussion. We decided we were done when each horse had ignored me twice as I lifted the bucket to them. I grabbed a towel to dab at where

I'd spilled water down the front of my show shirt and breeches while Karen lugged the giant water containers back to the truck. We returned to the group to find that I would be staying with Charleigh while Jessie and Karen took the other two horses back. Francisca (who had missed today's show because her daughter had a sleepover and her house was crawling with 10 year olds while we were loading the trailers early this morning) would meet them at the barn to help unload the horses and get the trailer back to pick up Lady Luck. It'd take about an hour and a half.

The trooper left. The woman with the Hummer and the peacock tattoos left. Jessie and Karen left. Charleigh tried to soothe Lady Luck, who remained agitated for any one of a number of reasons: we were standing still and she was in a trailer, there was grass outside the trailer, she'd been bumped and thrown around, and Xavier was gone and she was in love.

Then a truck pulled into the rest area behind us. And stopped. Behind us.

A muscular young man in a sleeveless t-shirt got out of the truck.

"Is there a problem, ladies?" he asked.

"Someone hit us," I volunteered. "Well, actually, someone hit Charleigh's truck, but I was in the other truck, but I was going to stay here so that if Charleigh needed help with anything..."

"Carol. Shut. Up," Charleigh said, looking up from her cell phone, where she was dialing a tow company.

The young man bent over near the crumpled fender.

"Looks a mess," he offered cheerfully. "Everyone OK?"

"I have to speak quietly," I whispered. "She's a bit upset. Her favorite show horse is in the trailer."

"Oh," he said, wiggling a piece of the fender. "You can't drive this," he added, straightening.

Charleigh walked over. "I know," she said. I'm trying to call for a tow."

"I'll give you a tow," he offered. "My mother has horses, and my father would want me to help you. That's why I stopped. I thought of my father."

I beamed. Charleigh, who has long honey-colored hair and blue eyes, smiled non-committally.

"I might even be able to straighten the fender enough so you can drive it. Right now it's rubbing on the tire too much, you'll shred it. It's good steel, I can't bend it without tools."

Charleigh nodded and I kept beaming.

"I'll go get a sledgehammer and chains. I'll be right back. Wait right here." The muscular young man hopped into his truck and waved.

Charleigh looked at me. "I'm not sure that having a stranger tell you that he's going to go get a sledgehammer and chains and will be right back is a good thing."

I had stopped beaming. "It does sound like a horror movie, doesn't it?"

We started laughing nervously. Well, I started laughing nervously, and Charleigh sort of winced at my laughing.

"We're going to draw straws," I said. "The winner sits in the truck ready to dial 9-1-1. The loser waits for Mr. Sledgehammer and Chains."

Charleigh looked at me. She stared. Usually, that stare wilts the feistiest horse, the most willful teenaged rider, and the most out-of-control horse show parent.

But I was fueled by sheer terror of a guy with muscles, chains and a sledgehammer. I've read too many of Rex's creepy murder mystery books.

When the guy with the big truck and scary tools returned, I was parked in the cab of Charleigh's pickup. My finger was poised to press the final "1" and complete the emergency call. I had the window down a little bit so I could hear any threats.

What I heard was an offer of a soda. Mr. I Have Both Muscles and Sodas asked Charleigh where "the older lady" was, because he had brought a drink for me, too.

I knew the sodas were drugged. He was undoubtedly going to maim, murder and dismember us AFTER drugging us into submission. Charleigh accepted a bottle of her favorite fruity soda and smiled winningly at Mr. Muscles, who casually walked over to his truck, pulled an enormous sledgehammer from the bed, and sauntered over to Charleigh's damaged vehicle. Where I was hiding.

"Here," he said, and started beating her truck's fender. My finger hovered closer to the "1" which would complete the sequence "9-1-1" and bring the law to rescue us. Charleigh sipped on her soda, nonchalant.

Just then Jessie came back with her trailer. I emerged from the truck, ears ringing from the hammer blows against the fender. I pretended I'd dozed off in the front seat after a long day at the horse show and the muscular guy with the hammer woke me up with the banging. And that I hadn't been crouched over a cell phone ready to dial 9-1-1.

Charleigh and Jessie unloaded Lady Luck from the damaged trailer and loaded her into Jessie's trailer, where Lady Luck sniffed and snorted and looked everywhere for Xavier, because the trailer certainly smelled like he was nearby and she was, as I mentioned, in love. I tried to give Lady Luck water, because that's what I do. She refused to be distracted from looking for Xavier.

Charleigh sent me off with Jessie and Lady Luck. I think she'd heard enough about Rex's murder mysteries. Charleigh stayed with the muscular guy, who had noticed Charleigh's tidy figure showcased by riding breeches, and was flexing his biceps and waving the sledgehammer around with great abandon. He wasn't the first. To notice that Charleigh is pretty cute, that is. I'm not aware of anyone else who expressed appreciation by waving a sledgehammer.

Lady Luck remained irritated and in heat until she finally made it home. Where she was still in heat, but not quite so irritated.

Charleigh limped the truck and trailer back to the barn, with the muscular young man following to make sure she was OK. She offered him one of the brownies in the tack room and a tour of the barn, both of which he accepted. Then she offered me as a tour guide.

I think he was a little disappointed. But he seemed to like the horses.

But at the end of the day, we reached our destination with all of our parts mostly intact, and completely failed to get maimed with a sledgehammer. So I'd call it a good day. (Even if Lady Luck and Mr. Sledgehammer-

and-Sodas were both, for their own reasons, a little bit disappointed.)

DRESSAGE

The dressage training scale is often arranged in a pyramid, with "rhythm" at the wide bottom of the pyramid, forming the base, and "collection" at the apex. While not a rigid format, it illustrates the levels a horse builds on as training progresses.

A SYNCOPATED RHYTHM

(According to the United States Dressage Federation's Glossary of Judging Terms, "rhythm" is "the characteristic sequence of footfalls and phases of a given gait. For purposes of dressage, the only correct rhythms are those of the pure walk, pure trot and pure canter (not those of amble, pace, rack, etc.) Not to be confused with "tempo," "cadence" or "miles per hour.")

Patience is a virtue. Horses teach patience. Or they try our patience. Or something like that.

For example, I became interested in dressage when I determined that my maturing sense of the ridiculous - as well as my aging legs - would no longer allow my plump, middle-aged behind to rise into jump position while I negotiated even a crossrail, no matter the size or courage of my mount. I was retiring from going over anything higher than a pole on the ground. I was becoming a dressage rider!

First, I needed to learn rhythm, a fundamental of dressage riding. I tried counting out loud, like Diana the Fearless. She could ride anything. Diana went from jumping to dressage when her horse topped out at 3' 6" and that height became routine. Diana's talented and athletic mare Daylily then began learning dressage moves and the duo quickly became known for their breathtaking tests, punctuated occasionally by a spirited leap when Daylily decided to return to her hunter/jumper roots.

Diana suggested I count out loud to improve my rhythm. Charleigh, my trainer, expressed amazement that I could count in complicated rhythms instead of steady ones.

"Consistency, please," Charleigh would demand, standing in the center of the ring while I trotted Bea around the perimeter, counting.

"One... two... three... four..."

A pause.

"Five. six...... seven... eight...... one two..."

"I think you have a syncopated rhythm going on there," said Charleigh. "Or something." She wasn't smiling.

Charleigh had me practice marching in place in the viewing room, counting while I marched. She didn't smile then, either.

"Match your feet to the counting, not the counting to your feet," she coached me.

I could do that. Eventually. But in the saddle, I continued to bow to Bea's lead and counted based on her footfalls, which sometimes marched to a palsied drummer, adding and changing beats based on random bars of sunlight or unexpected stacks of feed bags or the odd sparrow darting past. It was Springtime, and Bea's fancies had definitely turned to... well, if not love, then at least something other than dressage tests.

"I think she'll settle down when she's not in heat," I ventured to Charleigh, who would have none of my nonsense.

"Nonsense," Charleigh said. "That mare is always in heat. Circle. Get that horse to pay attention to you. You have to take the lead." She was obviously getting frustrated; her eyes looked like they could shoot lasers.

Thirty-two circles later, Bea and I were still establishing a rhythm. It was definitely reggae. But it was a rhythm, and it was better than before, so I decided to live to ride another day. I began walking to cool Bea out.

Karen came into the ring with her big dark gelding, Storm Trooper. Their lesson was scheduled following mine. Karen is easy-going and smiles a lot. Storm Trooper is beset by demons. Some days he's high, some days he's got the energy level of a houseplant. A small houseplant. That doesn't get enough sunlight. Storm Trooper keeps Karen guessing.

I dismounted and, while loosening Bea's girth and adjusting the stirrups, I watched Karen and Storm Trooper.

It was a houseplant type day for Storm Trooper.

Karen, her smile becoming slightly strained, was urging him forward and Storm Trooper was protesting. Karen carried a short crop. Nudge, kick, smack, head toss. Nudge, kick, smack, head toss. Nudge, kick, smack, head toss.

They had a rhythm going. A consistent, smooth, non-syncopated rhythm. I passed Charleigh on the way out of the ring.

Nudge, kick, smack, head toss. Nudge, kick, smack, head toss.

"There's a nice consistent rhythm," I whispered imprudently to Charleigh. "Nudge, kick, smack, head toss."

I was glad that her eyes couldn't REALLY shoot lasers.

RELAXATION
WITH ELASTICITY & SUPPLENESS

(Per the United States Dressage Federation, "relaxation" can refer to the horse's mental/emotional state or to the horse's physical state, which often go hand in hand.)

(WARNING: This article contains stereotypes which the author now knows are not accurate but are included anyway, as she considered them to be fact at the time these events took place. The author pleads that she was raised in a Midwestern state and personally knew a significant number of genuine cowboys, with genuinely bowed legs from riding horses for hours. They shared their cowboy wisdom with her, which consisted of grizzled versions of "Old Wives' Tales," and she, being of an impressionable age, believed them. Mostly because they had horses, which made sense to her at the time. Therefore, the opinions voiced in this section may be ignorant, ridiculous, and certain proof that I am not acquainted with your amazing Thoroughbred/Quarterhorse/Morgan/Draft mare/gelding/stallion.)

Bea is mostly Thoroughbred, which I understand is a hot-blooded type of horse bred to go fast, and this seems a bit sneaky because she's registered as a Quarterhorse, which is a breed of dependable and calm horses used to control cattle according to my first riding instructor, Farmer Norton of W____, Minnesota (who put me on his Shetland ponies and taught me to duck under branches on trails). This apparent sneakiness is aided and abetted by the American Quarter Horse Association, which registers Quarterhorse/Thoroughbred crosses, even when they're three-quarters Thoroughbred and only one-quarter Quarterhorse, as Appendix Quarterhorses. I didn't understand what Appendix Quarterhorses were when I made an offer for Bea, because I wasn't paying attention. I thought it was a line of Quarterhorses, or a type, like "Lippett" Morgans. Charleigh, my trainer and the owner of Flying Horse Farm, where I ride, was helping me shop and did not enlighten me. She frequently underestimates my ignorance, which I have tried to correct by illustrating that ignorance at every opportunity. When my modest offer for Bea was eagerly accepted (a bit disconcerting) and I checked Bea's registration a bit more closely, I discovered that she's the granddaughter of a famous racehorse (a Preakness winner!) and the Quarterhorse part of her background is somewhat buried. Except on her registration papers.

Ah, the perils of naiveté!

But Bea was schooled in dressage, so, shortly after she arrived at Flying Horse Farm, her new home, I began practicing the Intro Tests A and B. Not Intro C, it had cantering. And I was petrified, having just discovered that I now owned a mare (shudder!) with a lot of Thoroughbred (Oh no!) blood and a heritage of going very, very fast.

Charleigh began encouraging me to relax. She showed me the Dressage Pyramid of Things To Do and it included Relaxation With Elasticity and Suppleness.

I began doing yoga. I worked really, really hard to relax. Karen, one of the instructors at Flying Horse and an experienced horsewoman, told me to breathe. Then she told me how important it is to relax, and how the horse senses all my tension. So every time I got on Bea, I worried about relaxing. Bea pranced. I hyperventilated. Bea didn't walk, she jigged. My forearms tensed.

"Elasticity," Charleigh said in one of my first lessons with Bea. "Move with her, don't stiffen up."

The parts of me that were moving at all felt like elastic in a bathing suit that had been left in the car, in the sun, for a very long time: stiff and crumbly.

"Breathe," suggested Charleigh.

Easy for her to say. She hadn't bought a THOROUGHBRED, by accident, because of the sneaky registration practices of a certain breed association that is known for having NICE QUIET CALM horses. I practiced and practiced, working very hard to relax.

Anyone notice a problem here? I, of course, continuing to illustrate my ignorance, did not.

Finally, months after committing to Bea, Charleigh took us on a trail ride to benefit a cancer charity. It was a pretty big group, broken up into about twenty-five groups of just a few horse and rider pairs each. Bea relaxed when I finally got too tired to be tense. She chewed on the bit meditatively and kept a watchful eye out for panthers, and bears, and wolves, and trees with funny-colored leaves.

She channelled her Inner Quarterhorse. And I stopped blaming the American Quarter Horse Association for being tricky, and started blaming myself for being tense. About seven miles into the ride, I had a revelation on relaxation: If I am tense, my horse thinks there is a reason which she does not see. She does not imagine that her rider would be tense because of anything she is doing, as anything she is doing is eminently sensible. Therefore, danger must be lurking nearby.

So I'll just have to <u>force</u> myself to relax... hmmm... I wonder how well that'll work....

CONNECTION

(The United States Dressage Federation describes "connection" as "the state in which there is no blockage, break or slack in the circuit that joins horse and rider into a single, harmonious, elastic unit.")

My trainer, Charleigh, keeps nagging about "connection." Whatever that is. When I ask her, she says it's when the horse has all the parts connected, and when the rider is connected to the horse. She explains that it's like holding hands, only through the reins.

When I ride Bea, I check for connection. I never see any parts scattered around the ring. All her parts always seem connected to me. A nose here, an ear there, both attached to her head. One leg in each corner of her body. And I generally stay on, so we're connected.

I try to be a good student, but I think I put the Amateur into the "Adult Amateur" category. Sometimes Charleigh refers to me as an Amateur Adult Amateur, which I consider gives me a "triple A" rating - that's good on Wall Street, right?

So I keep asking Charleigh about connection.

Then Bea strained a ligament bouncing around in the pasture and spent a month in her stall recovering. Three weeks into her rehab, I was hand-walking her daily and taking her out to graze for a few minutes to relieve her boredom. Then I decided to try teaching her tricks. I'd done this with Schooner, an enthusiastic, slightly scatter-brained Morgan I'd leased for a few years, and it helped him focus. I thought it would give Bea something to do.

I showed Bea a ball, conveniently fitted with a handle that a horse could (theoretically) use to pick it up (Schooner had always just crammed any bit of the ball he could into his mouth and happily carried it around, looking like a vastly oversized vegetarian terrier with hooves and a funny tail). Bea just stared at me with her cat-like "Why did I have to end up with the stupid human?" expression.

I held the ball toward her. Bea continued looking at me and rolling her eyes. Not in fear. More like the wife in a television sitcom when the husband finds his reading glasses on his head after looking for them for an hour.

I put a little piece of carrot on the ball. Bea ate the carrot off the ball. I pressed the clicker I used to show her that what she is doing is correct. Then I had to give her another piece of carrot.

That, she understood.

Touch the ball. Click. Carrot. Repeat. A lot.

Finally, after about fifteen repeats, touching the ball wasn't enough. Bea had to nudge it, while it was on the ground. And make it move.

She did. The third time she rolled the ball several inches, I clicked, enthusiastically rubbed her neck and shoulder, and dumped several carrot pieces into her feed bucket. That signals the end of the session, and the horse is supposed to happily munch the snack reward while I gather the clicker and toys.

That day, Bea just looked at me. She didn't move away from the ball. She stood over it, touched it with her nose again, and then looked at me.

I rattled the carrot pieces in her feed bucket. Enticingly. She ignored me, and the carrots. She looked at her ball again, then back at me.

I got it.

Connection!

Bea knew what she wanted, and wanted me to understand. Which I did: I was to continue with the snacks and entertainment. Which I did.

We were connected, at last.

Just not exactly in the way Charleigh wanted.

IMPULSION

(This is another dressage term. It means "increased energy and thrust." The U.S. Dressage Federation explains it as "releasing of the energy stored by engagement. The energy is transmitted through a back that is free from negative tension and is manifested in the horse's elastic, whole-body movement." In a horse, this comes from the hindquarters, and there are many articles and books on how to make this happen.)

I figured out one method of creating impulsion very, very early.

In the little town by a lake where my grandparents vacationed, the "Five and Dime" store was the epitome of commerce. That's where everyone went for everything from toothpaste to motor oil.

And, in front of the store, a white mechanical horse arched its neck, frozen in mid-prance (hindquarters tucked, definitely in an uphill frame). Adorned with a gilt saddle and a silver bridle, its luxurious mane froze in wind-tossed waves as though stirred by an energetic gallop. A little box topped a pole next to the magic pony, with a slot to insert coins.

At age three, I was curious, and it was a horse, so I had to examine it carefully. My grandfather, because he was my grandfather and didn't have to live with me or take me shopping ever again if he didn't want to, happily placed me on this fantastic creature, dropping a coin in the slot.

Euphoria.

He was my grandfather. What were a few coins to make his first grandchild, she of the red-gold curls and snub nose, light up with the beatific smile seen mostly on saints' faces in stained glass windows? I must've ridden that horse for twenty minutes, never letting up on the smile, until his pocket change was exhausted. I was saddle-sore and my face hurt when I got off, but I was smitten.

And I knew about quarters: that's what makes the mechanical pony go.

Impulsion: it comes from the quarters.

My first dressage lesson.

STRAIGHTNESS

(Defined as "proper alignment of the horse's body parts from poll to tail. Directness of line of travel.")

The concept of straightness seems, well, "straightforward" - but it's not. And it's not natural, but it is good for the horse. Nature would allow the horse to travel crooked, aided by a natural tendency to be stronger on one side than the other (just like humans) and also to have larger hindquarters than chests (just like THIS human). These physiological features encourage a horse to move crookedly, eventually going lame, naturally, and, once again naturally, becoming food for a wolf or cougar. So I'm not necessarily a proponent of all things natural for my lovely mare Bea, and I worked to improve both her straightness and mine.

Which is a challenge. Responsive and athletic, Bea walked straight and balanced when we moved down the center line of the ring.

And then Charleigh, my frighteningly competent trainer, told me to ride circles and stay straight.

This is beyond comprehension. "Curves" and "straight" are not the same and not even similar. Had Charleigh never read a fashion magazine? Women have hair that curves and curls, or hair that is straight, and whatever type they have, they want to learn how to have the other type. Fashion abhors both excessive curves and excessive straightness, but they are NOT the same, just both undesirable.

Nope, Charleigh has obviously never studied a women's fashion magazine.

"Keep her straight!" she barked at me as I was guiding Bea in a circle at the far end of the ring.

I frowned to show Charleigh that I was concentrating and randomly flailed my legs. This does NOT work with Bea, who gets upset when I confuse her – in her world, flailing legs equals shouting, which is bad - and she starts looking for things to justify spooking. She's pretty athletic, so when her ears start pivoting toward patches of sunlight and a bucket that wasn't positioned there yesterday, I know I'm in for some flight time if I don't settle down.

Bea focused on a suspicious-looking damp spot in the ring. I stopped flailing and decided that it would be less terrifying to, once again, admit my ignorance. I guided Bea to Charleigh and stopped. Charleigh arched an eyebrow.

"How can I ride a circle and keep Bea straight?" I asked. "Circles are curved and straight isn't."

"Is that why you were flailing around?" Charleigh asked.

"Yes," I said. "I thought if I did something I might accidentally do the right thing."

"How is that working for you?" Charleigh fixed a gimlet eye on me.

"Not well," I admitted. "And Bea doesn't like it, either."

"No, she doesn't." Charleigh took a deep breath. "In horses, straightness means that their hind legs follow the track of their front legs. They can do that going in a straight line or in a curve." She squatted and smoothed a patch of the ring sand. She drew a couple of simple diagrams, showing me where the horse's feet traveled when the horse was trotting in a circle but had that mysterious "straightness."

"You can just ask if you don't understand, you know," Charleigh said to me. Then she cracked an uncharacteristically corny grin. "Be... straight with me!"

I groaned and turned Bea back to the rail.

COLLECTION

(DEFINITION: In Dressage, increased engagement, lightness of the forehand, self carriage. The horse's frame is shorter, with the neck stretched and arched upward. The tempo remains nearly the same as in the medium or extended pace.)

I recently rode in the indoor ring during a rainstorm. It was during the peak time for lessons, when Charleigh the owner/trainer, Karen the gentle and chatty instructor, and a raft of after-school lesson students populated the barn. But Bea needed her rehab exercise, and a day full of meetings and commitments carved my day into slivers, and this was the only sliver large enough to accommodate Bea. And outside was wet, so we mingled with the lessons and tried to stay out of the way.

One of the benefits/downsides of riding when Charleigh is giving lessons to other people is that she'll bark out an instruction, not necessarily gently, when I don't even realize she's noticing me. But Charleigh can tell, from the back barn with all the lights off and her eyes closed, if I'm posting the wrong diagonal or if Bea is cantering on the wrong lead.

I think she's magical. Or possessed. Or something.

Today was no exception. One quick glance in my direction, and Charleigh called out to me.

"Carol! You're hanging on each other! Shorten your reins! Drop your hands! Drive her forward! Sieg heil!" (I may have misheard the last bit.)

Another glance in our direction, as I'm dropping my hands and driving Bea forward and trying to sieg heil. "Her nose is sticking out and her butt's in another state! Pull her together!"

Well, OK. If I knew how to pull her together, I would. And I was pretty sure her butt was right behind mine. We're in a small state, but it's not THAT small. I was excited because she seemed like she was trotting forward briskly, with a nice rhythm. So I hadn't been expecting all that correction.

Jessie walked into the ring to talk to Charleigh. Jessie is one of two very accomplished adult amateurs at the barn. She retired with her fabulous Selle Francais gelding Xavier from hunter/jumper shows to dressage when he developed a crack in his hoof that finished his very successful jumping career. Jessie stood by Charleigh and watched the lesson students, and me. She whispered something to Charleigh. Charleigh called out to me.

"Shorten those reins! Her nose is in Alaska and her butt's in Hawaii!" And I'm in New England, I thought. I'd rather be in Hawaii. I wondered if I could trade places with Bea's butt. I shortened the reins, and kept Bea trotting. We had two minutes of trot left to go for her rehab exercise program.

Charleigh told her student to walk and cool out. She said something to Jessie while they both looked at me. Jessie said something back.

"Did you say something NICE?" I asked them. Jessie, as an experienced Adult Amateur, was usually very kind to me, an Inexperienced But Aspiring Adult Amateur.

"Yes," said Jessie.

"OK. Say it loud enough so that I can hear the good stuff, too."

"They sure look better than they did a year ago. Bea's hanging on the bit instead of going behind it," stated Charleigh, loudly.

"Thanks," said, unimpressed by THAT compliment, and still keeping Bea circling at the trot.

One of the students led a handsome Morgan gelding past the door. Bea saw him. She arched her neck, pricked her ears and lightly danced the next three trot steps. Bea is a terrible flirt.

"Ooh! Bea saw a cute boy! Now THAT's self-carriage!" barked Charleigh. "Make her do that all the time!" she ordered.

"Bring on the cute boys and I will," I responded, and brought Bea to a walk.

So the secret to collection is a cute boy passing by the ring? Well, it is for Bea at least...

LESSONS LEARNED

Some horses will test you, some will teach you, and some will bring out the best in you.
> -Inspirational poster

Of course, some will place you on the ground... maybe not gently...
> -Voice of Experience

TRAINING SAM

An article in a recent equestrian publication breathlessly listed the amazing feats of the latest trainer-of-the-month. He's ruggedly good-looking, I'll give him that, and he knows how to wear a cowboy hat. He even looks like a country singer in some of his promotional photos. In a lot of them, in fact. And he can OPEN A GATE while MOUNTED ON HIS FAVORITE HORSE!

I didn't know that was such a big deal.

My little gelding Sam and I could do that, when I was fourteen years old. Without a saddle. Or a bridle. Or even a halter.

And without even knowing it was an amazing feat.

I grew up in a very rural area of a very rural state in the middle of the Midwest. My parents indulged me with a happy childhood. That, for me, had to include a horse. I got Sam, a very cute but otherwise unexceptional green-broke two-year-old (what were we thinking?!) for my thirteenth birthday. We kept him at a nearby farm owned by Mr. Johnson, a retired-cowboy-turned-farmer, complete with bowed legs and a sense of humor. He probably saved my life, multiple times, because I didn't know what I was doing.

Sam lived with a small herd of horses in a giant pasture. He didn't wear a halter, because he was outside in a huge area all the time. If he got it caught on something, he'd likely be in trouble long before he was found. The horses were expected to be able to be caught, and they were. Mr. Johnson put up with very little nonsense from his horses (but a great deal of it from me).

Heavy with facts from innumerable magazine articles and every horse book in every public library within fifteen miles, I was ignorant of one thing: how truly ignorant I was. For example, Sam was green broke. I thought that meant that I just needed to ride him a lot. Also, the summers in the middle of the Midwest are very hot. I tried to ride with shorts on, found that shorts are incompatible with saddles and spent two weeks nursing raw sores on the insides of my thighs. I ditched the saddle. Bits seemed cruel, because I was thirteen years old and didn't realize that bits are only cruel when hands are harsh. I ditched the bridle, and rode in a beautiful leather halter with flashy parade reins. The halter was for taking a cow to a show, and, if I pulled back suddenly, it rode up Sam's face and the earpiece sagged over his tiny and perfect ears, leaving only a small headshake between riding with a headstall of some type and riding with nothing except legs, seat and my voice. Each of which would be clutching, bouncing or screaming, because Sam was likely to be running.

But it was a very handsome halter, with shiny brass fittings which I lovingly polished, and so I accommodated. I only tugged on one rein, and only when Sam decided that running, at his speed and in the direction of his choosing, was the wisest option. When I couldn't put a stop to whatever ridiculous activity Sam had started, I put the right rein under my foot and pulled. I'd learned that from a magazine article. It did tend to slow Sam down, and it did keep the cow halter on his head, but I developed a bad (and enduring) habit of responding to all emergencies, real or imagined, by unconsciously pulling with my right hand. I trained my hands to be harsh - at least my right hand, much to the dismay of my current trainer, who has spent countless lesson hours reminding me to drop my right hand and relax it.

Getting Sam from the field was easy. An unexcitable sort (unless a pheasant erupted beneath his nose or some other emergency came up), Sam usually ambled toward me as soon as he saw me. I rewarded him with a carrot, and would hop on his back to ride out of the field. We had to pass through two gates, and we learned to open them and close them without the bother of dismounting. Through my seat and legs, I could place each of Sam's feet where I wanted them, and, being a compact and athletic sort, Sam seemed to enjoy the challenge of understanding my commands and following them.

At least he did until I tried to use less tack. A halter and one lead rope were almost as much equipment as I used to ride in on the roads and trails that comprised our wanderings. So I tried just a lead rope, and looped it around Sam's neck. That was fine, and we opened and closed our gates and walked and cantered up the hill out of the field.

And then one day I kept the lead rope tied around my own waist when I hopped on Sam. He stood for a moment. I urged him forward with my legs, turning my body to direct him. He went forward, but did not turn at my direction. He ambled purposefully toward the nearest tree and very slowly and very deliberately scraped me off. I got back on and tried again. Same response. I put the lead around his neck, and Sam obediently followed my direction.

I guess he wanted me to put at least a little effort into our partnership.

TRICKSTER

Childhood television programs weren't necessarily educational. At least, not in a good way. I had been seduced by Fury racing to his human, Mr. Ed having companionable chats with Wilbur, and various trusty steeds who reared, galloped or performed amazing feats for their human companions. And I wasn't the only child who was hoodwinked.

My girlfriend Ruby was surprised on her eleventh birthday with the ultimate surprise for a horse-loving pre-teen. Her father led her favorite pony, Magic, up the driveway and handed her the lead line. She'd adored this pony for a year. She had ridden Magic for lessons and braided dandelions (which is what ten-year-olds mean when they say "wildflowers") into his mane. Then, in a fantasy fulfilled, he became hers.

Ruby took to pony-ownership immediately. She taught tricks to Magic. Ruby had watched Fury on television. She taught her friend to rear on command. He got a treat when he reared. Pretty soon, he enthusiastically interpreted the slightest movement as his cue to rear - and get a treat.

This gave Ruby a problem. When she wanted him to go forward, he reared. When she wanted him to back up, he reared. It got so that anything she asked of him brought about a rear. Magic never unseated her, and never reared higher than necessary to make a good enough show to earn that treat, but it was a habit that Ruby knew she'd have to cure. Magic's enthusiasm was getting to be real troublesome.

Ruby asked everyone she could find how to fix her problem. An old cowboy laughed and laughed when she explained what she had done, and then told her to break a raw egg between Magic's ears whenever he reared. It would, he assured her, make the unruly pony think that he'd hit something with his head and the egg running down his face would feel like blood. He'd lose his enthusiasm for rearing. Ruby took to carrying eggs in her jacket pockets. She had a few mishaps, with broken eggs leaking all over her clothes. But in about a month she did cure Magic of rearing. And, thanks to all the scrubbing to remove the raw eggs, he had a very clean and lustrous mane and forelock!

And Ruby began teaching her dog tricks, and stuck to just riding Magic.

JOSEPHINE AND HER CURE FOR FEAR IN THE SADDLE

Josephine is a pretty, delicate professional woman. She is soft-spoken and fairy-like. When you meet her, you sort of expect sparkles and glitter to dance in the air around her.

Josephine started horseback riding as an adult, and has been taking lessons for about a year. Admittedly timid, she was part of a small group of Barn Chicks (adult women who love horses and hang around the barn rather than shop for shoes) discussing what makes people take up horseback riding as an adult.

"The challenge," stated Diana, who is very sure of herself.

"I think it's the thrill of danger," offered Jessie. "And the challenge of competition."

"I know I'm terrified," stated Josephine. "Horses are pretty scary."

Diana started lecturing Josephine on ways to get over fear. I think Josephine was supposed to take certain vitamins, wear a shirt with an open collar, and breathe in a special (and quite complicated) pattern based on the time of the day or the phase of the moon or something. Josephine, Jessie, and I were getting glassy-eyed trying to keep track. Diana was sure this would solve everything.

"I'm always a little afraid when I mount up," I interjected. "That's part of the attraction. Like riding a roller-coaster or jumping out of an airplane."

Josephine's eyes lit up at that. "I want to jump out of an airplane," she said, her voice wispy with excitement.

I was going to have to re-think Josephine. She carries a delicate, fragile aura totally at odds with an enthusiasm for skydiving, which I refuse to do because I'm afraid I'll throw up or otherwise embarrass myself.

We discussed the merits of being in a team sport with a

member of another species, inter-species communication, the joys of making a big hairy guy actually do what you want, the fun of getting out of the house and into someplace dustier and smellier than home - we all had something to offer.

Josephine stopped the show when she piped up, in her sweet voice and with her gentle smile. "The other day I took out a nice little motor scooter that my brother has. I've always liked to ride it, but I was pretty scared of it. I hadn't ridden it in over a year. But this time, I wasn't scared at all, it was just fun."

"Cool," said Jessie.

"I guess that riding horses re-set my fear threshold, and now the scooter doesn't seem at all scary," continued Josephine, eyes bright.

"That's interesting," I said. "Your view of the world has changed."

"Yes," breathed Josephine. "Now I think I'm going to

take up bull riding so I'm not afraid of horses anymore."

She didn't laugh, or even smile. She looked eager.

That's definitely a new side of Josephine.

CONFIDENCE

Charleigh the Horse Goddess, who owns Flying Horse Farm and gives riding lessons, likes to coach me on confidence. "Shoulders back" she'll snap. "Head up." "YOU made him spook. Stop looking in that corner and expecting him to act up!"

Well, one day I developed confidence and certainty in my equestrian abilities and goals. Much to Charleigh's dismay.

We were going to a hunter pace. This is a type of competitive trail ride that mimics field hunting, only without actually hunting anything. A set trail is marked out, with the type of obstacles (fences, ditches, streams) one would find in a field hunt. Fences can be avoided, and safety is stressed. A group of experienced riders test the trail and establish a fast, but safe, time. None of the riders of the hunter pace know what that "ideal" time is until after the competition. Riders go out on the course in groups of two to five, usually. There are no standardized rules for all hunter paces, except to stay on the course. Prizes are awarded for coming closest to the Secret Correct Time. It's all a bit like gambling, to me, but I consider it an excuse for an organized trail ride, with lunch afterwards.

Our destination was an elegant hunt club. There would be ten miles of well-kept trails, followed by an elaborate catered lunch, with wine, under a tent reminiscent of a wedding reception. We'd been instructed by Charleigh, who had arranged the outing, to dress as though we were showing and be sure to not wear any red, as it was reserved for the officials of the hunt club (she kept looking at me when she said this, because I'm finally convincing her of my ignorance of English Riding Etiquette). Francisca and I were to ride together, and Karen and Joy were a team. Charleigh would be there, driving the horse trailer, but would not be riding.

An idyllic setting: gentle hills undulated between rock walls, golden in the early sun. We drove past kennels of energetic hounds. They jumped and barked behind high fences.

After our little caravan of horse trailers and a minivan arrived at the hunt club headquarters, Karen asked Charleigh if the dogs were actually used for field hunting, and she nodded.

"They use a scent drag," Charleigh explained. "Field hunting with live animal prey was outlawed in Great Britain years ago, and has been discouraged in this country. But this club is quite traditional, so they do have hounds."

We went to the registration tent and picked up our packs, including the numbers we were to wear and our lunch tickets. We paused and admired the giant rosettes that would be awarded later. Then we unloaded our horses, touched up their grooming (we'd polished and braided them the night before) and tacked.

Riders in formal hunt attire - including the officials' red jackets - dashed everywhere. Horses called to each other. Excitement thickened the air, almost palpable.

My cheerful gelding, Schooner, started to dance. I remembered learning in grade school that horses are colorblind, but every time Schooner saw a red jacket he bounced on all four legs. I chose to think he was bouncing with eagerness. For the first time, I was entering an equestrian competition with a personal sense of calm.

Francisca and I mounted, and went to the starting area. We followed Karen and Joy, who left without a hitch (although Joy was chewing her lower lip and threatening to hyperventilate). Francisca, on Jack, a rangy gelding, smiled gently with her Zen-like calm. Schooner bounced because he saw another red jacket, one that I hadn't even noticed.

We passed the starting line and our timed ride had begun.

Before leaving the main area, the course took us up a small rise. Schooner, eager, had set a walking pace that was quicker than some of his canters. We were halfway up that first rise when I heard a scuffling, a

Very Bad Word, and a thud, followed quickly by thundering hooves. Jack dashed by, reins flapping, without Francisca.

Suddenly, I was riding a camel. A one-humped camel with very, very stiff legs. I idly wondered if this was the rounded back so desired by experienced riders, and dismissed that thought. This wasn't a rounded back, this was a keg of gunpowder. Schooner had decided that anything that set Jack off was probably very frightening indeed, and only my (now, sadly tense and unconfident) riding was keeping him from joining his companion, who was dashing through what looked like a Royal picnic, with beautiful tents, decorated tables and shiny vehicles.

Meanwhile, cries of "Loose horse! Loose horse!" spread among the tents and tables. Francisca responded to my questioning call that she was fine. Schooner marched, stiff legged and uncertain of my sanity ("It's time to RUN! This is ESCAPE time!") to the nearest knot of people, who were searching in the direction that Jack had gone, wringing their hands.

"Is there anyone here courageous enough to hold this horse while I get off?" I asked. Two people declined, rolling their eyes in a manner I'm certain mirrored Schooner, but one gentleman, in a red hunt jacket, stepped up. Schooner had continued his stiff-legged gait, and finally stopped under the man's sure hand, despite the red jacket.

I dismounted from Schooner's camel hump. I took Schooner, who was indeed rolling his eyes, to find Francisca. She was walking, stiffly as Schooner, up the little rise. We could see Jack in the distance, circling the registration area. Charleigh was walking in that general direction.

Charleigh caught Jack, of course. She brought him back to us and handed him to Francisca after inquiring about any injuries.

"Get back on," Charleigh said to Francisca. "Jack has finished his self-lunging and he'll be great now. He probably ran about three miles."

Then Charleigh turned to me. "Mount up!" she said.

"No," I said.

"What?" she asked, incredulous.

"I am not riding that horse," I explained. He's all wound up." I felt pretty confident of this.

Charleigh looked at me. I looked back. I am significantly older than she is, not that it intimidates her in the least, but it does give me some feeling of security.

She sighed. "Want me to school him for you?" she asked.

"OK," I said. "But I am not riding that horse in this hunter pace." Confidence!

"You have to," she said. "Francisca needs a teammate."

"You ride him," I said.

"I don't have a helmet," she said.

"Here." I handed her mine.

"It's too big," she said.

"It's adjustable," I answered, confidence building. "And you always tuck your hair up so you'll need the room."

"I don't have boots." She looked at me. "And your boots are definitely too big."

I nodded. "You have paddock boots on," I said.

"If I ride that far without tall boots, my calves will get all chewed up."

I just looked at her.

"I'll go school him," Charleigh said. "And then you can get back on." She had a lot of confidence, too.

I held Schooner while she got on. My confidence was corroding.

Charleigh took Schooner off to the side. We'd collected a little audience. Schooner was performing. If he was a Lipizzaner in Austria's Spanish Riding School, we'd call what he was doing "Airs Above the Ground." Charleigh called it "Behaving Badly." Finally, he settled into walk, trot and hand gallop. Lots of hand gallop. The man in the red jacket next to me commented to a woman in a red jacket.

"He's quite a handful, isn't he?"

When the woman agreed, my confidence soared again. I was NOT riding that horse in this hunter pace. Charleigh was.

I turned to the people next to me. "Is there a place where I can get a pair of half-chaps to fit her?" and I nodded in Charleigh's direction. She and Schooner were hand galloping in a giant circle past the parked trailers.

"Because I am NOT riding that horse in this hunter pace," I added confidently.

The man in the red jacket looked me up and down. I could see him mentally comparing my middle-aged physique against Charleigh's toned and taut rider's body. "I have a pair of my daughter's half-chaps with me. She can borrow those."

"I will give you my first-born," I offered. "Or my second-born. Or both," I added generously.

"That won't be necessary," he responded rather seriously, and went to get the half-chaps.

Charleigh returned a few minutes later with a sweaty and only slightly subdued Schooner.

"Here he is," she said, hopping off.

"I am not riding that horse in this hunter pace," I said, with confidence.

"You can't leave Francisca alone," she protested.

"You'll ride," I said. "I am not riding that horse in this hunter pace." Confidence.

"I don't have tall boots," Charleigh said.

I handed her the half chaps. "I borrowed these for you."

"I was planning on working while you were riding," she said, weakening.

"I'm sorry," I said agreeably. "I am not riding that horse in this hunter pace." Retaining and building on my confidence.

Charleigh put on the half chaps and swung back in the saddle. Schooner tossed his head and rolled his eyes, and our little gathering of red jackets and others stepped away from the energetic Morgan, who was reminding them why they owned warmbloods.

An hour and a half later, I watched for them at the finish line. Francisca wore the smile of a Madonna. Jack sauntered, loose-jointed and relaxed, definitely giving the impression that HE was the star of their group. Schooner walked woodenly next to him. Schooner's hair formed wet whorls and spikes. Even his mane lay plastered to his neck. He smelled like the losing locker room after the Super Bowl - lots of sweat and lots of upset.

Even Charleigh looked worn out.

"Have a nice time?" I asked, not too cheerily. I knew better.

Charleigh peeled herself from the saddle and peeled the borrowed half chaps off her legs.

"Take these back," she said. "And then get back here and take care of your horse." I didn't have the guts to remind her that the horse officially belonged to her. She glared at me, energy crackling so fiercely I expected sparks from the wisps of hair escaping the helmet, and continued. "If there had been a trailer going to an auction at the halfway point, this horse would have been on it."

I returned the half chaps and gushed gratefully, but quickly. The man in the red jacket had ridden, and returned with a bloody nose from going over one of the fences with enthusiasm. He was getting a lot of attention for it, and someone kept trying to hand him a silver flask. My gratitude wasn't allowed to distract everyone from the heroism of a possibly broken nose.

I felt like I was in another country.

Until I returned to Charleigh, and handed her the cold soda I'd fished from one of the many refreshment tubs. I'd debated over a wine cooler, but knew she wouldn't drink alcohol, whatever the amount, before pulling a trailer full of horses. Charleigh accepted the soda and thrust the reins into my hand. She stalked off, probably in search of her usual composure, which had definitely gone missing. I haltered Schooner and tied him to the trailer. He'd calmed into exhaustion the instant I'd taken him off Charleigh's hands.

I glanced sheepishly at Francisca. "I hope I didn't ruin your ride," I apologized.

Francisca grinned broadly at me as she covered her saddle. "Oh, no," she replied. "Charleigh even said you made the right choice. About halfway through the ride, we had to cross a stream. She said he was awful, and you probably wouldn't have stayed on. Keep it between us, but even Charleigh wasn't finding him easy. Poor thing, he was really scared."

My confidence swelled like a crescendo in The New World Symphony.

I was right.

REX RIDES!

My wonderful husband, Rex, is tolerant of my hobbies but shares few of them. Notably absent from the short list of "Things We Do Together" is horseback riding. A couple years after the midlife crisis that led me back into the horse world, I bought Rex a gift certificate for a riding lesson. I thought it would be fun to watch him, even if a light bulb didn't turn on above his head as he realized horses were the missing component in his life, now that he was married to the perfect woman and had two marvelous children. I'd seen Rex ride once, on a Rent-a-Horse Trail Ride many years ago when we were dating. I remember him saying "Whoa, Buck, steady there, Buck" pretty much the whole ride. Buck was in no danger, at any time, of breaking a sweat in spite of the warm and humid weather. Rex, however, had been sweating quite a bit.

Charleigh, the owner and trainer at Flying Horse Farm, put Rex on twenty-seven year old Romeo, a once-fashionable Morgan who was retired and happy in his role as Beginner Horse Who Must Never Go Fast. Rex clambered into the saddle and Charleigh led Romeo around the ring while Rex chanted his mantra ("Easy, there, Romeo. Steady, boy. Easy there...") and I snapped photos. Charleigh spoke soothingly to Rex until he relaxed into Romeo's very easy and very steady and very, very slow rhythm.

Charleigh then introduced the trot, and posting. The rhythm of posting was a bit beyond Rex, who dances like a man who earned a Math and Economics double major in college (which he did). But Rex sat the trot as though he knew what he was doing.

I complained.

"How come he sits the trot better than I do? I bounce around a LOT more. And I've had a lot more lessons, and a lot more experience."

Charleigh responded to me, still in a soothing voice, "Because Rex is not leaning forward and perching like you tend to do."

"I try not to," I defended myself.

Now, a barn is an earthy place. There is manure, and naked horse parts, and horse bodily fluids, and other such things that are not usually discussed at dinner in polite circles. One becomes a bit immune to this, and some of the jokes are even a bit crude. But Charleigh was not joking; she was consoling me and explaining my lack of ability in an area where Rex shone.

"Yes, but leaning forward makes it harder to sit the trot. Rex has boy parts, so he naturally won't lean forward. He has a built-in negative feedback if he does." Charleigh spoke in a matter-of-fact manner. She was just instructing a student.

For an instant, I thought Rex was going to pass out and fall off Romeo. His boy parts just don't get mentioned casually by young women with honey-colored hair, rose petal skin and baby blue eyes.

I wish I'd gotten a picture of Rex's face. And I could never get him on a horse again. I think he was afraid that his boy parts would be, once again, casually discussed.

But he won't talk to me about it.

DIFFERENT JOBS

I've seen horses working, and I've seen horses without work. They seem happier with a job, at least a job they can understand and do - like many have at Flying Horse Farm, where I keep Bea. One elderly gelding (try to say THAT ten times fast!) enjoyed his job as a lesson horse so much that, when Charleigh, the barn owner, put him into retirement because of his stiffening joints, he listlessly mouthed his hay and moped about in his paddock. After a month during which Romeo began to drop weight and lose the luster from his once-shiny coat, Charleigh put one of his favorite young lesson students on him. In spite of legs that defy the laws of physics by still holding him up, Romeo began the elderly horse version of prancing, neck arched and ears alert. Following the lesson, he waited for the bits of carrots and the gentle pats that were his due for a job well done. That evening, he ate his grain and hay with gusto and, during his turn-out time, interacted with his pasture mates. For two years, Romeo has been out of retirement. He has a job: to give pleasure to young horse lovers and care for them while they learn to ride.

Another working horse is a lovely mare imported from Iceland. She is delicate and beautiful, with a lot of blond hair, dainty hooves and melting brown eyes. Gentle and quiet, Hera delights all who see her, including her devoted human, Sara. Hera lives at Flying Horse Farm, and one day I happened upon Hera and her human sharing a moment.

Hera stood in the aisle. Sara was brushing her dreamily to a haunting melody coming from a CD player carefully set up on a folding stool. A small cooler sat next to the well-organized grooming box. When I greeted her, Sara started and turned to me, looking sheepish.

"I didn't know anyone else was going to be around," Sara stammered. "This is embarrassing…"

Sara is a highly educated professional woman. She's been in scientific research for many years, and is sent around the world on complex projects. Hera is her hobby, her relaxation. When she is at the barn with Hera, she focuses entirely on enjoying her horse. So seeing Sara nonplussed put me in the same condition.

I smiled at her in a questioning manner and arched an eyebrow.

Sara straightened and indicated the CD player, the cooler, the brushes, the small plastic bowl with an assortment of carrot and apple pieces and saltine crackers. "You must think I'm nuts," Sara said.

"No, I don't," I said firmly. "Are you enjoying yourself and Hera?"

"Yes... I am... " Sara answered, slowly and with the skepticism of her profession.

"Then I think you are enjoying your horse and she is doing her job. And I think you pay her bills," I explained.

Sara threw back her head and laughed.

Hera does indeed have a job, and she excels in it.

Another resident of Flying Horse Farm, Choco, is a squat brown horse with a quiet demeanor. He wasn't always quiet - before his young owner outgrew him, they competed in junior eventing, where they danced around in a dressage ring and sailed over obstacles both in a ring and outside. His teen-aged human's legs grew long enough to trouble them over jumps and she arranged to have him stay at Flying Horse Farm as a lesson horse.

Choco found himself challenged to understand different riders. He gradually found his niche as a specialist with timid beginners who found his small fuzzy ears and short stature comforting, with an occasional foray into working with a more accomplished rider learning dressage or jumping.

Lynn and I had bathed Bea in preparation for a show and were letting her graze in a tasty patch of grass near Choco's paddock while she finished drying in the sun. I held Bea's lead rope and Lynn kept me company.

"Did you see Choco's new halter?" Lynn asked me, pointing to the dirt-colored pony. He had been standing in the sun, relaxed, almost dozing until Bea's appearance caught his attention. I looked and started to laugh. A bright pink nylon halter, heavily decorated with hearts and flowers and "I love Choco" messages in various colored markers hung crookedly on his head.

"Let me guess," I wheezed between guffaws. "Riley Simms, right?" I named one of Choco's latest conquests.

"Yep," Lynn nodded. "Wonder how long it'll take before Choco finds enough mud to roll in to tone that color down?"

Choco continued to look at me, head down, neck relaxed, halter crooked, the picture of a long-suffering recipient of an excess of pre-teen affection who also knew he deserved it and all the carrots it entailed.

And he sighed. Deeply. "The things I put up with for carrots," he seemed to say.

Don't we all, Choco. Don't we all.

SHOPPING? UGH!

I don't much like shopping. For anything, really. But I thought I'd like shopping for a horse when my husband Rex and I decided the time was right for us to add an equine to our list of dependants (which, with our sons Bing and PJ on their own, we had whittled down to Toby the Wonder Cat, Dr. Evil Cat, and two fish I'd inherited when a friend relocated across the country and I've forgotten the names she had for them so I call them "Spike" and "Old Guy").

Many years ago, as a teenager, shopping for a horse had been wonderful. I'd had more fun than a shopaholic with someone else's credit card watching late night television infomercials. Until my father got tired of carting me from farm to farm every weekend and bought one of the horses while I wasn't paying attention.

This time I was more goal oriented, and I hated, with every fiber, riding a strange horse in front of a group of horse people. It didn't matter that they wanted me to like the horse and buy it. It didn't matter that I'd probably never see these people again. It didn't matter that I wore a moustache disguise and gave a fake name (well, I didn't really, but I did consider it). So I hired Charleigh, my trainer and the owner of the barn where I ride, as my Personal Shopper. I felt pretty cool about that - it was like having someone pick out the colors, sizes and styles of clothes for me to try on so I didn't have to wade through racks of items. At least I wouldn't be riding so many horses, in front of so many people.

So I gave Charleigh my requirements. I wanted a gelding, and I wanted him to be a draft cross so he'd be sturdy and wouldn't go lame and break my heart like Schooner did. I didn't want him to be too tall. The ground wasn't always soft, so I wanted it at least to be fairly close. I wanted to ride on trails, and maybe go to an occasional little show, and generally hack around. He didn't have to be handsome, or excessively smart. And NO THOROUGHBREDS and NO MARES because I had deep prejudices and was scared of them.

Charleigh began giving me horse ads off the internet. She found an American Warmblood mare named Mabel who looked promising, except for the "mare" part. I drove Charleigh out to look at Mabel, and when we pulled into the driveway, Mabel was hanging her head over a paddock gate and I started bouncing around in the car.

"You need to drive," said Charleigh. "Stop bouncing."

"But that's Mabel! Right there!" Somehow seeing her in person was like a celebrity sighting. After all, I'd seen her photo on my computer screen, which is sort of like a television, so it seemed exciting to actually see her in real life.

"Yes," Charleigh said, in the tone of voice she uses to indicate my excuse is unacceptable.

In a short while, I was formally introduced to Mabel, a large, calm and handsome mare with the solid build of a Barcalounger. I realized I would have to ride her. In front of both Charleigh (intimidating) and Mabel's current owner (almost as intimidating). Luckily, Mabel was privately owned and not boarded in a stable crawling with young girls who jump three foot high fences and don't need to know about the special equestrian undergarments that prevent cellulite from showing through riding breeches.

I made the owner ride Mabel first. Then Charleigh did. Then finally it was my turn and I clambered, inelegantly, into the saddle, using the picnic table in the corner of the riding ring as a mounting block. (Me: "Do NOT get up until I'm on or this thing will tip over and Mabel will kill me!" Charleigh: "Yes, I know." Hardly reassuring.)

Mabel's owner watched. Charleigh gave me pointers, most notably "Breathe." Mabel and I walked, trotted, and cantered in each direction. Charleigh kept frowning. I wasn't sure if I'd upset her or if she was thinking. I wished I had brought cookies for Charleigh. Sometimes cookies distract her from the fact that I ride like an orc from Lord of the Rings. Mabel's owner didn't seem to mind my riding much, but after all, she did want to sell me her horse. Charleigh and Mabel's owner talked. I couldn't hear them, and I was kind of glad. I tried to concentrate on Mabel.

Finally, I got off. Charleigh asked questions. I helped put Mabel away while her owner showed that the horse wasn't afraid of anything by scratching her on the hindquarters with a manure fork. Mabel liked it.

In the car, Charleigh asked me what I thought.

"She's nice," I ventured. "Should I buy her?"

Charleigh rattled off a long list of concerns that revolved around equine body parts that I knew belonged to a horse but didn't know for sure where they were located or what they were supposed to do. I knew roughly in which body quadrant they were located, but that was it. Apparently she would want a full pre-purchase veterinary examination. But we were getting that anyway.

"What does that mean?" I asked, pretending that the driving was distracting me. We were on a straight road, in the country, with beautiful weather and no traffic, not even a stray squirrel.

I hadn't fooled Charleigh. "It means you're looking at other horses, too," she explained.

Charleigh scouted through countless internet videos and rejected most of them for "hitchiness in the right stifle" or "looks not quite right in the front - maybe a shoulder thing" or "hocks, definitely hocks" or any other of a myriad of mysterious lamenesses. She finally settled on an Appendix Quarter Horse mare named "Douceur" that we would visit. I did some research, too. I found out that "Douceur" means "sweetness" in French and is pronounced "Doo-sair." It sounds better when a French person says it than when I do. I didn't check to see what an "Appendix Quarter Horse" is. It's a Quarter Horse, right? And they are calm and stocky and not very tall.

Douceur resided in a barn inhabited mostly by lanky

warmbloods who looked down their slightly Roman noses at the 15-3 hand mare with the broad chest and ordinary coloring. No blaze, no stockings, no chrome at all, just a reddish-brown bay dwarfed by the latest fashions in hunter-jumper breeds.

"Plain," I thought. "And small. But she's a Quarter Horse! And I like Quarter Horses!" I didn't notice the gleam in Charleigh's eyes as she looked over Douceur. We saddled her. Douceur pretty much ignored me and everyone else during the process. Mabel hadn't been warm and cuddly, but Douceur made her look like a Care Bear. Douceur did perk up when her owner, a petite and lovely Frenchwoman dressed like an equestrian supermodel cooed her name and elegantly fished treats out of the pocket of her designer riding jacket. Otherwise, Douceur ignored all of us.

One of the trainers bridled Douceur and put her through her paces in the stylish indoor ring. The ring was actually paneled and decorated with silhouettes of horses hanging far above horse level. Then Charleigh lept onto Douceur. I didn't notice the drool spot on the front of her jacket, but I did notice that Douceur danced. They made a lovely picture together. Of course, I'd seen Charleigh ride an elderly Morgan with an attitude problem and make him look like a champion, so I wasn't surprised that Douceur had morphed into a vision of equine loveliness under Charleigh.

Charleigh got off Douceur and handed me the reins. "You try her now," she said.

I led Douceur to the mounting block and clambered into the saddle. I rode her at a walk, trot and canter in each direction, under Charleigh's watchful eye and terse tutelage. I brought her into the center of the ring.

"She has a big canter," I said. By which I meant that I had felt pretty much out of control.

"She has a lovely canter," said Charleigh.

"Lovely and big," I responded, what remained of my confidence eroding.

"Not that big," said Charleigh.

I gave up trying to sound like I had a clue. "Should I buy her?" I asked. She wasn't exactly a draft cross gelding, but I was tired of shopping already.

"Maybe," said Charleigh. In the car on the way home we discussed Douceur's merits. I was concerned that she was fast, but Charleigh dismissed that concern by telling me I was tense.

"Yes," I answered, and changed the subject. "Why are we looking at mares?"

"Because that's what is available," Charleigh said. When I went onto the internet, there were a lot of geldings for sale, and I mentioned that.

"Because mares are what I'm finding that are sound and within your price range and within a hundred miles of us." Since I myself couldn't evaluate soundness without a lameness vet and my checkbook, I accepted that.

The next horse we were to see, the following weekend, was a gelding. An off-the-track Thoroughbred gelding.

"A Thoroughbred?" I asked. "An EX-RACEHORSE THOROUGHBRED?"

"Yes," answered Charleigh, and I knew enough to shut up and drive to see "James Bond."

Thoroughbreds intimidate me. They run fast. They are bred to go fast, and trained to do only that if they are destined to race. And James Bond, cute name notwithstanding, had raced. I was not sure about this venture, in spite of the photo on this horse's ad showing him in a field of daisies with a slender young woman wearing a fluttering, gauzy top. At least he didn't look fierce and competitive there.

We arrived at the stable and met James Bond, who was already saddled. Charleigh examined James while I petted him and scratched his withers.

We tried him - first his owner rode him to show us, then Charleigh rode, briefly. When I rode, I started at the walk and was ready to stop after once around the ring. My inexpert seat registered a problem, and I couldn't steer the horse. He wobbled off to the left and I felt as though I were driving a car with a broken tie rod (an exercise I don't recommend and never intended to do and hope I never repeat). I obediently walked and briefly trotted in each direction and got off.

"He's... very sweet," I said, grasping for the description everyone uses when they can't think of anything nice to say. But he <u>was</u> sweet, and nuzzled me gently.

I turned to Charleigh. "Should I buy him?" I asked. She looked at me with her steady gaze.

"No," she said. "We are going to look at the two mares again."

We visited Mabel again. I liked her. She looked like she could carry me easily, muscles laying thickly over a sturdy frame. A ruddy bay, her coat glowed with health and a white blaze accented her kind face.

Should I buy her?" I asked as we drove away.

"We're looking at Douceur again," Charleigh replied.

We did. Charleigh rode her first, and gathered a large crowd. Douceur's owner had apparently told people we were coming. I heard Charleigh humming as they trotted past me. Humming means she's happy. Her audience watched raptly, with occasional murmurs of appreciation. Finally, Charleigh brought Douceur to a halt in front of me. Various members of Charleigh's audience, which by now included two trainers, three stablehands, the owner of the barn, six boarders, Douceur's owner, the farrier, and two dogs, applauded.

"She's my trainer," I announced generally. "She's teaching me to ride. I'm the one looking at this horse." I was afraid to try to pronounce "Douceur," so I didn't say her name.

Douceur chewed on the bit and her ears fell to the side as the applause quieted. Douceur was waiting for further guidance from Charleigh, the Horse Goddess. Charleigh vaulted lightly from the saddle and handed me the reins.

"Your turn."

I looked around, wanting to wait for the crowd to disperse, but they didn't. Charleigh, relentless, told me to mount. I did.

Douceur walked and trotted and cantered in one direction. Once again, her canter left my stomach about six strides behind. We changed direction. Walk, good, trot, good, canter... oh my! Wrong lead.

"You're on the wrong lead!" hissed Charleigh as we careened past her. "Back to trot!"

I couldn't. The tighter I held on to the reins, the faster Douceur went. Every time we got within hissing distance of Charleigh, I heard about it, but I couldn't do anything about it. So I circled Douceur, counter-cantering. Nothing. Tighter circle, and then even tighter. Finally she broke to a trot. I stopped in front of Charleigh, whose eyes were glowing, and not in a good way. I could see the red tint through the haze of the smoke coming out of her ears.

"Never. Do. That. Again."

I looked at her quizzically.

"You NEVER use tight turns on a horse that is counter-cantering. You have GOT to get some control!" Charleigh was pretty excited, and in that not good way. But I'm older, and not as easy to intimidate as I once was. But I was humiliated. Charleigh had attracted a crowd, and they had stayed to watch me ride, not a Valkyrie, not National Velvet, but a Troglodyte in a dressage saddle.

"I tried," I hissed back. "But my training is lacking in how to get THIS horse to slow down. Maybe I need better lessons." That usually stops Charleigh, since she's the one supplying said lessons.

Charleigh smiled at Douceur and patted her. Douceur looked generally unconcerned about everything. We took her back to the cross-ties, untacked her, and asked a couple of questions of her owner. I absent-mindedly draped an arm on Douceur's back and scratched her withers, encouraging her to make silly faces to show her appreciation. Douceur obliged.

"Eye will leev you for a minute to talk," said Douceur's owner. She vanished down one of the aisles.

"Should I buy her?" I asked Charleigh.

"She's a nice horse. You could make an offer."

I could be done shopping! But...

"Will I ever be able to ride her? And stop her?"

"Of course," answered Charleigh. "You did ride her – and stop her - today, didn't you?"

"Eventually," I admitted. I gave Douceur a final pat and wandered in search of her owner. I found her, and made an offer.

"Will Charleigh be zee trainer?" she asked.

"Yes," I answered.

"Will Charleigh ride Douceur sometimes?"

"Yes," I answered.

She threw her arms around me and accepted my offer.

I was done shopping! And I had... a mare. But at least she was a Quarter Horse!

And then I found out what an Appendix Quarter Horse is...

(NOTE: The American Quarter Horse Association has created a special registry and numbering system for qualifying Quarter Horse-Thoroughbred crosses. These horses are considered Quarter Horses, but are named for the registry system created for them — "Appendix." And, please note that I eventually did overcome my preconceived notions regarding Thoroughbreds as well as mares and am happily aware that all horses are, indeed, individuals.)

LEAP OF FAITH

OK, it wasn't really a "leap," just figuratively. When discussing horses, a "leap" usually implies more than an idiom - but this time, it was just an expression...

I was riding my new horse, Bea. She's got an accelerator, but she is not too interested in slowing down. Every horse has subtleties, and Bea's seemed to all lead to one place: go faster. If you touch her with your right leg, you want her to go faster. If you tense up, you want her to go faster. If you lean forward, you want her to go faster. If you lean backwards, you want her to go faster. If you lose one earring, you are unbalanced and she should (of course!) go faster. Basically, her cue translator is stuck on "go faster." I hadn't yet found the instant "whoa." In fact, I sort of had to plead for a while about "whoa."

Charleigh, the barn owner and trainer (who I privately think of as "Charleigh the Horse Goddess" because she has an uncanny understanding of horses and she frightens me a little bit), told me that Bea went faster because I was tense and Bea thought that meant there was something scary nearby. Of course I was tense, I was riding a horse that always wanted to go fast. Charleigh said I could ride as fast as Bea could run, so I should relax about it. I tried, and got tense about not being able to relax... which made Bea want to leave the area and my source of tension, whatever it was... quickly.

Although Bea is registered as a Quarterhorse, she's actually an Appendix Quarterhorse which basically means she's part Thoroughbred (the rules are actually more complicated than that - but I won't try to explain everything here, mostly because I don't really understand them). Anyway, there are all sorts of racehorses in Bea's pedigree, and there's even a Preakness winner on her mother's side. I find that somewhat intimidating sometimes, although it's also kind of cool. But I'm getting ahead of myself. Bea is well put together with nice gaits, and seemed personable, and I hate shopping, even for horses, and Charleigh liked her, and Bea's owner immediately accepted my first offer. Suddenly I had Bea the Energetic in my one-horse string.

And, two months later, a nervous Amateur Adult Amateur (that would be me) is sitting atop a nervous Bea the Jigging Appendix Quarterhorse... and I was trying not to grit my teeth, counting the minutes until this ride would be long enough not to be embarrassing and counting the months until the magical time when Bea and I would "settle in" and "become partners" and all that mystical nonsense that I was seriously depending on.

Meanwhile, Charleigh was in the center of the ring, giving a student a lesson. "Nice," she said, quite kindly. "Take a walk break."

"Carol," Charleigh said. "Drop your reins and ride on the buckle."

"Are you kidding?" I thought. "This horse is jigging and just trembling to take off. If I even loosen the reins, we'll be running laps until next Tuesday." I figured I didn't really know what Charleigh meant. Maybe I have the wrong definition of "drop your reins and ride on the buckle"...

"Carol," Charleigh said, with exaggerated patience. "Drop the reins."

I ignored her again. I was behind her, she couldn't see me, and I love my husband Rex and our two sons. I wasn't ready to spend the rest of my days paralyzed and attached to a ventilator.

"Carol, drop the reins." Charleigh's voice sharpened. She was entering Charleigh the Vengeful Horse Goddess mode, and her eyes had started to spark.

I was about to ask her to tell Rex he should remarry so Bing and PJ would have a mother, even though they were hardly little children any longer, when Charleigh spoke again.

"Carol, DROP THEM!"

I took a deep breath and released the reins, gingerly holding them between one thumb and forefinger. I was more scared of Charleigh the Horse Goddess than of Bea the Jigging Wonderhorse.

Bea immediately sighed, dropped her head and slowed to a relaxed walk.

I sighed and relaxed, too.

How did Charleigh know?

Like I said, sometimes she scares me.

ENGLISH AS A SECOND LANGUAGE

It has taken me years to figure this particular thing out. Many, many years. And my mare Bea has been working very hard to help me understand, but I have been slow.

Horses understand English. At least some horses, including my Bea.

During a recent lesson, my trainer Charleigh was reminding me to loosen my shoulders, drop my right hand, and engage my core. For the umpteenth time.

"Will I ever remember this on my own?" I complained from on top of a very patient Bea. "You've told me this umpteen times."

"You will," said Charleigh. "Maybe after I've told you umpteen and one times."

Bea snorted. Charleigh laughed.

"She's stating her opinion," said Charleigh.

"Which I don't appreciate right now," I replied, dropping my right hand another fraction of an inch.

A few minutes later…

"Drop your right hand and loosen your shoulders," coached Charleigh.

"My core's engaged?" I asked hopefully.

Before Charleigh answered, Bea shook her head. Bea never just shakes her head at the trot, unless we're outside in warm weather and there are flies. Or unless we're inside, like today, and she's making a point.

"I agree with Bea - it's not," laughed Charleigh. "But I didn't want to give you too many things to think about at once. Your shoulders are less tight, and your right hand isn't as high as it was, but it's creeping up."

Bea tossed her head, very slightly. (I am not making this up.)

After the lesson, I dismounted and chatted with Charleigh for a moment before leaving the ring. Bea always seems to enjoy this time and pays attention to our conversation. Frequently it's about how wonderful she is.

"She certainly gave her opinions today," I said, scratching Bea on her withers where she is always itchy.

"Bea was quite expressive," agreed Charleigh, and rubbed Bea's neck. Bea half closed her eyes in ecstasy at the stereo stroking.

"Do you think she understands English?" I asked. Bea opened her eyes wide and, I swear, rolled them. Charleigh laughed.

"I think so," she said.

Later I told this story to my animal-loving friend Ruby. Ruby can get wild chipmunks to eat from her hand and has even taught a fish to do tricks. Kind of lame tricks, but a fish isn't equipped to play fetch or shake hands, so I shouldn't be too picky. Ruby pointed out that if I were taken care of by another species, and pretty much at their mercy, I'd concentrate on understanding what they said even if I couldn't speak.

I guess she has a point. I can just see Bea rolling her eyes at me... again...

GENEROSITY

Sometimes teenage Barn Chicklettes (as we call the young girls who hang around the barn like Fashionistas at a Manolo Blahnik clearance sale) surprise us with their grace. And not just in the saddle. Amber, one of the more accomplished (and competitive!) Barn Chicklettes proved that graciousness can be acquired at a young age...

Amber wants to ride everything with four legs. Her family Saint Bernard was in constant danger of being saddled (with a small towel) and ridden over jumps when she was in preschool. The dog wasn't very cooperative, but Amber kept trying. By the time the girl hit Middle School, she was riding everything in the barn and begging to try any new horse that came in. She wanted to jump higher and gallop faster and score better. This girl loved to show, and by age thirteen, her volatile moods depended on the color of the ribbon she won at her latest show, be it a recognized event full of polished competitors or a (relatively) scruffy schooling show. Amber lived to compete.

I began to complain good-naturedly about riding against her in schooling shows. Ribbon color is vastly important in my world for about forty-five seconds, and then I pretty much forget. But it's a lot of fun to tease Barn Chicklettes.

So when I bought Bea, I made arrangements with Charleigh, the barn owner and lead instructor, to make her available to certain upper level students for lessons. Sometimes I'd be out of town for several days at a stretch, and if selected riders took lessons on her, I'd know Bea would be getting well-supervised exercise.

Amber was first in line begging to ride my lovely and talented mare. I wasn't there for Bea's jumping debut with Amber, and when I rolled in to the barn the following day, Amber greeted me with the enthusiasm only a thirteen-year-old girl infatuated with a new horse can display (You think you've seen excitement with a thirteen-year-old girl who has just met a cute new boy? Ha!).

"Charleigh let me jump Bea! I rode Bea for my lesson and Charleigh let me jump her!" Amber was jumping up and down, without a horse.

"Cool! Was she a good girl?" I asked, encouragingly.

"She was wonderful!" enthused Amber. Then she quieted, suddenly. "But I thought she was pretty tricky. I told Charleigh that you make her look easy."

I smiled. Bea is very well trained, very sensitive, and very responsive. If you wrinkle your forehead, she notices and thinks it's a cue for her to do something. Usually to speed up. Heaven forbid you actually apply firm leg pressure.

Amber continued. "Charleigh said that's because you 'get' her. Someday I'm going to be able to, too." And Amber bounced off.

Coming from a competitive, eager young rider, that's a very generous compliment - not all adults would be able to share so openly.

I made a batch of cookies for the barn that I know Amber likes. And brought them when I knew she'd be there.

And I carry a warm spot in my heart for Amber, and her innocent generosity.

LIFE AROUND THE BARN

If Heaven doesn't have horses, I'm not going.

– Heard around the barn

AND THROUGH THE WOODS

Charleigh, the barn owner and trainer, decided some of her many charges would enjoy a hunter pace. A hunter pace is a low-key competitive event based on foxhunting, but without a fox. And without the requirement to go over fences. Or to go fast. It's really an excuse to go on a trail ride, usually of several miles, on a trail that has been tested for horses. And there are ribbons, maybe even trophies. But the ribbons aren't based on speed, but on how close the competing teams get to the ideal time, which is determined earlier by a test team or two sent out by the event organizers.

So it's basically anyone's guess. But few people worry about the awards, really, and the riders of Flying Horse weren't going for competitive reasons. We'd be enjoying an organized trail ride, with an organized picnic lunch afterwards.

But Charleigh wasn't sure which horses would be suitable for long periods of outside riding in unfamiliar surroundings. So she started testing the horses.

Romeo, an aging Morgan gelding, had developed a reputation for being "hot" at shows - he pranced, danced, and acted a fool at every opportunity. And opportunities come thick at horse shows: trucks, trailers, other horses, unfamiliar humans, fluttering ribbons, unfamiliar trees, unfamiliar fences, unfamiliar grass... Romeo noticed it all, and each thing was a matter of concern.

But Romeo had put on a few years since his peak horse show days, and had mellowed. So Charleigh decided that Romeo, now a favorite in the lesson program among the timid crowd, would be among the horses considered for the hunter pace outing. But he had to be tested.

Enter Charleigh's Current Favorite Adult Guinea Pig: me. I had a riding lesson.

"You'll be riding Romeo today," Charleigh said.

"OK." I seldom got Romeo to ride anymore, but I

wasn't suspecting anything and just thought maybe my more usual companions were having a busy day with other riders. I brought Romeo in, tacked him, and went into the ring to clamber onto his sixteen hands with the aid of the mounting block.

"We're going to have our lesson in the outdoor ring," Charleigh said.

"OK." I turned Romeo to go out the door.

"The outdoor ring down below," Charleigh added.

"OK," I said, and then I started getting suspicious. "Down below," huh? I had heard rumors of Romeo's reputation. I was also very aware of Romeo's aging legs and joints, and didn't expect any antics that I couldn't ride through. But I was beginning to feel like I was participating in an experiment. Charleigh walked next to Romeo and me and spoke soothingly about my equitation (which she, uncharacteristically, praised highly - increasing my suspicion that Something Was Definitely Up).

We reached the ring and Romeo and I walked, trotted and cantered in both directions. Charleigh was never far away. After the lesson (in which I was praised much more than usual, corrected a little, and all in the gentle tones one would use to coax an ax-murderer into giving up his weapon), Charleigh said we were going to walk down the short trail that wound through the trees and led to the stream.

"OK." We were walking through Killer Trees Hiding Bloodthirsty Predators, according to Romeo. At this point, I knew for sure that I was on an experimental ride. But I actually felt pretty cocky. Charleigh had praised my equitation, it was a compliment to my stick-in-the-saddle skills that she was using me for this test, and Romeo was looking around and rolling his eyes, but he did that a lot, even when the color of the footing changed slightly, or he saw a mud puddle, or there was a white horse in his vicinity.

Charleigh walked with us, still speaking softly to both Romeo and me, as we walked into the trees. She paused and pretended she wanted to rest, motioning us on ahead. Charleigh never needs to rest.

"Go up that little hill and then come back," she directed us.

Really? She is so busted! Surely she can't expect me not to notice that now she wants to make sure Romeo can be controlled outside by an amateur without her soothing presence...

Romeo and I obediently walked up the hill, turned, and carefully returned to Charleigh. We began to walk back to the indoor arena, together.

"You are so busted," I said as we left the trees behind.

"What?" she answered, all blue eyes and innocence.

"I know when I'm being used as a test subject."

"You did very well," Charleigh answered.

"And you were testing Romeo with me because you know that if you get on him he'll be perfect but he might not be with one of us mere mortals."

She smiled. "That was a very good lesson" was all she'd say.

THANKFUL FOR BARN CATS

At Thanksgiving, my family likes to discuss the things for which they are thankful. When I said "barn cats" a couple years ago, no one else understood. No one else in my family spends much time at a barn. Barns have grain and sloppy horses. Mouse heaven. And the mice invite all their friends to move in, too.

Charleigh wanted to avoid barn cats. For some reason, she just didn't want them. She pretended that her Jack Russell terrier, Blackjack, would handle all vermin.

Blackjack did not. While he could hone in on a rat from thirty yards away and dispatch it with speed, he lacked the patience to wait for mice to emerge from their hiding places, so the mice just hunkered down while Blackjack was in the area and waited him out.

Jessie and I started bringing in little plastic containers of cat-pee-soaked kitty litter and storing it in the back of our tack storage cupboards. We hoped to discourage mice from using the convenient little rooms full of expensive leather goods as snack bars. Jessie even surprised a mouse party once, sending several small rodents scampering through whatever tiny crevice they used as an entryway. We tried to seal cracks and knotholes in an attempt to discourage their parties, but this proved futile.

Until some guy involved with a feral cat rescue group gave Charleigh a hard-luck story.

Raoul had four cats in a big cage in his garage. They had been captured, vaccinated and neutered. But they couldn't be returned to the patch of woods where they had lived, because it was now a strip mall. They'd been in his garage for five months. They weren't cute. The market for unfriendly full-grown cats with scars and a violent history is pretty small.

Charleigh's heart is big, and she's a sucker for a hard-luck story. She agreed to take the cats, and within a few hours there was a wire cage in the hayloft. Raoul worked fast. The cage was about the size of my first apartment. It had better furniture than my first apartment. And it had four crabby cats as residents.

After a month of acclimation and daily feeding (the food was at least as good as in my first apartment), they were released. Three stayed around. One, the prettiest (which means she had the smallest scars and almost all of both her ears left), took off and only showed up every month or so for a rest and a large meal. The other three graciously accepted names (Molly, Meggie and Sebastian), settled in, slept on hay bales, watched the scenery from various loft openings, and hunted.

We began finding mouse parts near the cats' food dishes. Sometimes they'd leave just a tail, like a trophy, as evidence of their work. Sometimes there was a body part that Jessie, who is The Goddess of Cats and a Mighty Fine Dressage Rider, insisted was a delicacy and thus a sign of respect and affection from the hunters. And which I couldn't even identify. Not that I tried very hard.

I never asked Jessie how she knows what part of a mouse is tasty. I don't want to know. (I'm slightly suspicious of her sinuous grace, her deep understanding of everything feline, and even her slanted green eyes. Sometimes it wouldn't take much convincing to have me believe she turns into some type of large cat when the moon is full, or quartered, or something.)

Now and again we would find an entire mouse, often artfully arranged. Jessie claims that she once found a mouse laid out with a corn kernel in its mouth and blades of grass around it, like parsley.

I think Jessie has a lot of imagination. Of course she does, she's the one who suggested the little containers of kitty litter with cat pee. Which we were able to stop using. Thankfully.

Blackjack still chases rats, and sometimes pretends to hunt for mice. As a Jack Russell terrier, living on a big horse farm, he just has too many things to chase to waste hours patiently watching and waiting for small vermin to show up.

But Molly, Meggie and Sebastian don't.

Thankfully.

BARN FOOD

Flying Horse Farm has a room that is heated, lined with cupboards assigned to individual boarders for tack storage, and filled with rickety tables and assorted chairs. There is a plexiglass window looking out onto the indoor arena. This room is like a clubhouse. Students, boarders, parents and an occasional vendor gather in what we call "the viewing room," talking, feeding coins into the vintage snack and soda machines, or peering out the (usually) smudged-with-nose prints window to watch children grinning during a lesson.

The viewing room is a repository for leftover Halloween candy, remnants of birthday cake, cookies, and giant jars of jelly beans. (One of the moms found out that Charleigh, the owner of the barn, likes jelly beans and picks up a gallon-size jug of them whenever she shops at her favorite warehouse store. These jars are quite popular and last about 4 days.) Sometimes someone brings a coffee cake, or even a fresh-baked loaf of bread, with butter and honey. Nothing lasts very long.

With one exception.

A new boarder arrived with her adorable young mare. Joy was eager to participate in the socializing that barns seem to foster, so one day she decided to contribute to the ongoing food festival in the viewing room. For a week, she tantalized us with promises of a special treat. She told us she was known for this recipe, and brought it to picnics and family gatherings. But she would not tell us what this was. Jessie, Charleigh, Francisca and I placed bets. Jessie bet a tub of chocolate-chip cookies from her favorite bakery that the surprise would be cream cheese brownies. Charleigh voted for cupcakes decorated with red licorice, because she likes both cupcakes and red licorice. Francisca thought granola cookies, because Joy seemed health-conscious. I suggested cheese and fruit, because I was convinced Joy was more health conscious than even Francisca thought she was. We all agreed we'd bring in what we'd bet Joy would, if we were wrong (except for Jessie, who doesn't bake and has the chocolate-chip-cookie connection).

The big day came. Joy brought in a cooler! I knew I'd won the bet. With some fanfare, Joy pulled out a covered tray sitting in a pan of ice. She unveiled the treat, her face glowing with pride.

Deviled eggs.

Charleigh doesn't eat hard-cooked egg yolks, no matter how doctored up. Francisca doesn't eat hard cooked eggs at all. Jessie and I gamely dipped in and tried them. They were delicious. Jessie smiled at Joy and nibbled on her egg. I scarfed down four, and I was done. Although they WERE delicious, I was the only real fan of deviled eggs in the area. Joy left the tray in the viewing room, carefully covered and sitting on ice, available for all to try.

Those delicious eggs sat in the viewing room until almost all the ice melted. A couple people tried one, but Faith, one of the teen-aged riders, summed up the prevailing opinion when she answered another teen's "What are THOSE?" with a grim "They are definitely not cookies." They could have sat there for weeks, if they wouldn't have spoiled.

Charleigh gave the remaining eggs to her husband, Phil, who enjoyed them very much. And Joy never brought deviled eggs again.

But Jessie brought chocolate-chip cookies, Charleigh brought red licorice, Francisca brought granola cookies, and I brought fruit and cheese. There wasn't a crumb left for Phil.

CHICKLETTE GAMES

Barns and horses are a source of a lot of entertainment. Not all of it involves riding. Or grooming.

Our "Barn Chicklettes" are the teen and pre-teen girls - and the occasional boy who is an "Honorary Chicklette" - who hang around the barn. They have a lot of energy. They play a lot of games. One of them is "What celebrity would this horse be if he/she were a celebrity?" Another is "What type of high school student would this horse be if he/she were a high school student?" These games are a lot of fun. Except I don't know the same celebrities. So I do better when I listen quietly than when I try to join in. But sometimes I forget that.

"He'd be Sean Connery," I say about the incredibly handsome grey Arabian who nickers suggestively at furry hats. At any furry hats, no matter who is wearing them.

"Who's that? Is he the guy that works on Saturdays?" asked Amber.

"He's a comedian, right?" says Martin, an Honorary Chicklette. "I've heard his name."

I explain to the Barn Chicklettes that he played James Bond. Originally. They shrug. He played Indiana Jones's father. They shrug again, then Lily brightens.

"Proty," she starts, naming a Morgan who is cute enough to be in cartoons and has a great deal of forelock, "would be J_____ L____!" She names a boy singer who probably doesn't shave yet but whose image graces innumerable fan magazines. Several Chicklettes squeal in agreement.

Wow. I would have placed Proty as Paul McCartney of the Beatles. But I knew better than to mention that. These Chicklettes probably didn't know the Beatles, and certainly didn't know Paul McCartney as anything but a mature singer - certainly not as the adorable young mophead who resembled the human version of

Proty.

When they reach twenty-one years of age, I'll give them a "leg up" ceremony, like the "Fly Up" ceremony in Girl Scouts when one graduates from being a Brownie Scout. They'll become full-grown "Barn Chicks." We'll have cupcakes and jelly beans, barn food staples.

And I'll explain to them who Sean Connery and Paul McCartney are. It's culture.

COOL BLUE STEEL: 194 HORSES

Horsepower sometimes comes in multiples, and sometimes we need horsepower to get us to the horses...

My husband, Rex, and I needed to replace our station wagon, which was starting to hint at imminent retirement. I tried to ignore the signs, because I hate shopping for just about everything. Especially cars. Especially with Rex. Although my father is even worse.

So I let Rex shop alone. He read, researched and roamed car lots. He shared brochures and magazine articles and all sorts of data with me, while I sat, glassy-eyed, at the kitchen table silently hoping for one of the boys to interrupt us. Or for a meteor to crash through the roof to interrupt us. My one contribution was to suggest a (choke!) minivan, because the boys were growing tall and fast and the backseat of just about everything is uncomfortable for the long car trips we take all too often.

Rex decided on a particular brand and model. He took me to the three dealerships within easy driving distance. I drove a minivan at each place. We talked with salespeople. I was done in twenty-four minutes. It took five hours. We had a good price, within our budget, with the dealership we liked the best and felt was most convenient. I told Rex we needed to go to lunch. At a diner. Over grilled cheese, I skillfully led him into a discussion of the minivans we'd looked at earlier. Then I skillfully suggested that we should make a decision. Then I skillfully went in for the kill.

"I like the teal one the best," I said to the still-wavering Rex. No way was I going through another Saturday car shopping. I'd rather have a Brazilian wax and a root canal. At the same time. From a gorilla.

"That one's nice," he agreed.

"Or do you like the dark blue one?" I suggested.

"No, that would show the dirt too much," Rex said.

"Then we'll get the teal one," I said, with great conviction. (Note: skills in use.) I stood up. Rex was long done with his sandwich, and half of mine. I popped the remaining corner of my half-sandwich in my mouth and picked up the check. "Let's go," I said, as I led the way to the cashier, dropping a tip on the table as we left.

Next thing Rex knew, we were in the car and he was driving to the dealership with the teal minivan. We bought it before we went home. Two days later, we had sold our station wagon to a neighbor who owns a car parts store (and laughed at me when I warned him that the make-up mirror on the passenger side was broken - after all, he owns a car parts store and doesn't wear make-up) and picked up the minivan.

I didn't drive it for a month. I am NOT putting the first scratch or the first stain on a new car. Finally, Rex stopped polishing it and admiring it, and I started to drive it. It's a minivan. Rex got tired of it and went back to his tidy little sedan with manual transmission. Much more fun. Much more macho.

And then Bing learned to drive. In the minivan. He had great incentive to learn to drive Rex's car, which is a manual transmission and most assuredly NOT a minivan.

Some of my friend's teens learned to drive in the minivan. Finally it was PJ's turn.

PJ defines "cool." He is easygoing, the adolescent version of a "man's man." He took to driving like he takes to everything, with easy mastery and a decided lack of drama. And if there's a lack of mastery, then PJ handles that with aplomb, too. In fact, if PJ never gets the hang of something, like figure skating or dressage riding, he'll handle that with good humor. PJ got his license with no drama. He drove for the first time on the highway, in bad weather, without complaining. But he was driving a minivan.

There's a conundrum. How can PJ, the Cool, drive a minivan?

He made it cool. One day at a lacrosse game, I overheard PJ talking with some friends. They were asking PJ if he was driving Blue Steel to some event.

"Blue Steel"?

Yep, my minivan was now improbably macho and cool. I actually saw a teenager with expensively messy hair and designer ragged jeans pat the teal blue (and slightly scratched) fender. "Blue Steel," she sighed.

By this time, I'd entered my Equine Mid-Life Crisis and was making regular trips to Flying Horse Farm, where I was taking riding lessons and eventually leased a horse. Blue Steel was perfect for barn trips. It was roomy for tack and definitely no longer new after years of car pools with sweaty soccer players.

One year I offered to drive friends from the barn to Equine Affaire, an annual trade show for horse enthusiasts that offered deals, and information, and clinics, and free little gizmos that you bring home to leave sitting in bags for months. I could take six people, if they were friendly and no one bought saddles at the show. They were friendly, agreed not to buy saddles, and I drove. We packed Blue Steel with coffee and donuts for the hour-plus drive to Equine Affaire, then filled it with horse paraphernalia from our bargain hunting (everything from saddle pads to strangely-shaped hose racks) for the return trip. The following year, I was asked to drive Blue Steel again. Someone else paid for the parking, others filled the gas tank, and my coffee and donuts were covered.

I felt like a celebrity.

Blue Steel was requested for horse shows, and hunter paces, and almost anything barn-related that involved a road trip. After eleven years of service, Blue Steel had racked up 320,000+ miles and served seven student drivers, including the DaVinci Madonna godchild, who launched Blue Steel into a parking lot and rocketed the minivan onto an unmarked island in front of a bank. Someone must have seen this; two days later the parking island was painted a bright, warning yellow. (Please note that the DaVinci

Madonna godchild started her driving career by launching a golf cart into the air, all four wheels, and giggling madly. I let her practice driving with me anyway...but I always double-checked my seatbelt.)

My - well, Blue Steel's - mechanic made a game out of keeping Blue Steel on the road. Not that it was too difficult - an oil change here, a set of tires there, and the minivan just kept running. Rich the Car Magician suggested that Blue Steel, at 300,000 miles, should be acknowledged by the manufacturer. I called the T_____ Customer Service line, then sent a letter detailing how happy we have been with Blue Steel. One enthusiastic voice message urged me to call back, sounding like I'd won the Publisher's Clearinghouse Sweepstakes, at the very least. I called back and spoke with a very bored customer service representative, who said my enthusiastic caller was out. Maybe out sick. Maybe with distemper.

A week later, I received a package in the mail from T_____ Customer Service. It was a glittery heart-shaped keychain and a notably ugly hat. I took the hat to Rich the Car Magician along with a box of donuts to make up for it. We laughed.

I never saw Rich wear the hat. But he doesn't hold it against Blue Steel. We're going for 350,000 miles, now!

And Blue Steel is still the ultimately cool minivan. And to PJ and his friends, and to my barn buddies, Blue Steel has become a legend.

FIREWORKS

The 4th of July is a tough day at the barn. Although we're in the country, of course, there are other rural dwellers nearby who bought their houses with the idea that all they'd enjoy would be pastoral views and sunshine and fresh air and chirping birds.

One such innocent bought a house with an elaborate back deck that looks out over our manure pile, which waxes and wanes with the seasons (a company in charge of fertilizing large tracts of greenery carts it away periodically). This manure pile has been there for forty years. The house is two years old, built on speculation. It had taken that house most of those two years to sell.

In February, when the prospective owners saw it and made an offer to buy it, the fields were covered with pristine snow, marred only by an occasional deer track. When they closed on the house and moved in, two months later, spring buds burst through rich soil and distracted them from their new view. Within three weeks of the first crocus blooms, the owner brought a bottle of wine and his dog to visit and meet the owners of the barn. He asked them, cautiously, if the manure pile would be there in the summer. Charleigh assured him that manure continued to be created year-round, even in the summer, by each of the thirty-two horses on the property. She said she thought he wanted to take the wine back.

The neighbor still has barbecues on his back deck, but he seems to serve a lot of adult beverages. And he burns a lot of tiki torches. And candles. And, on the Fourth of July, he lights a lot of firecrackers.

By dusk, everyone knows to be off the horses and have them safely back in their stalls, with hay. But sometimes Manure Pile in the Backyard Neighbor has a riotous party and they begin the fireworks even before dusk. It may be how he consoles himself.

One year, the fireworks started well before dusk. Horses began running in the paddocks, galloping in circles with every pop or boom.

Except for Schooner.

Schooner, a cute Morgan gelding with a crooked blaze and loads of enthusiasm for adventures, and treats, and attention, did not join the mad galloping. He perked up his little, well-formed ears and scanned in the direction of the fireworks. There was a party! He liked parties! At the next sizzle and pop, he began trotting toward the celebration.

Charleigh, the barn owner, was gathering the nervous horses and bringing them inside. She swears she heard Schooner ask for a lawn chair and a beer. She brought him in last, and firmly believes he was disappointed.

A few days later, Charleigh introduced Manure Pile in the Backyard Neighbor to Schooner, who performed some of his tricks (bowing, fetching a ball like a thousand-pound golden retriever, and pretending to drink out of a big plastic soda bottle). Schooner won his heart and the neighbor made peace with the manure pile.

FIREWORKS: PREPARATION

The Fourth of July is always an exciting holiday at a barn. Horses generally don't like flashes of light and sudden loud noises, be they thumps or crashes or booms or sizzle. Consequently, the riders at Flying Horse Farm are careful to be off their horses by dusk when the neighbors are celebrating Independence Day.

Except Jessie, running late, decided that dusk was far enough away for her to fit in a few minutes of preparation for an upcoming show and saddled her tall, dark and handsome warmblood gelding Xavier. They went into the indoor ring to run through a couple of dressage tests. She underestimated the neighbor's enthusiasm for all things noisy... and the fireworks started. Jessie tensed, expecting corresponding fireworks from Xavier.

A year before, Flying Horse Farm had acquired an active Morgan who had been sent to auction and garnered no interest except from the "kill buyers" who bought horses at bargain prices and sold them to slaughter. Monty was rescued and found his way to Flying Horse, where he attracted a lot of attention because of his story. He got used to the attention, and was practicing getting more of it by kicking his stall walls, sending a deep booming noise resonating through the barn. Everyone had gotten used to Monty's noisy demands, but not everyone appreciated them, particularly Jessie.

Xavier had gotten used to Monty banging whenever Jessie rode him in the indoor ring. Monty was very aware that Jessie carried carrots and distributed them generously. So whenever he knew Jessie was nearby, he communicated his eagerness for treats with an equine Morse Code of stall banging. It did not matter that Jessie was trying complicated dressage moves with Xavier. Monty felt his desire for carrots had priority. Over everything.

On this night, Monty was quiet but the neighbors weren't. When Jessie realized that Xavier was ignoring the deep booms of the fireworks, she relaxed and they finished their brief session before the neighbors began to set off the sizzling noisemakers. After the ride, Jessie and I talked while cleaning our tack.

"You know, they started the fireworks before dusk," Jessie mentioned.

"They did. It looked like a big party," I responded, dabbing more saddle soap on the pommel.

"I really expected Xavier to go crazy when the fireworks started."

"He didn't though - I'm surprised he was so calm about it."

"I wonder why…"

We both rubbed the saddles for a moment, contemplating.

"I think I got it," said Jessie. "Those booming noises sound like Monty kicking his stall."

"They do," I agreed.

"I bet Xavier has just gotten used to that type of booming noise," suggested Jessie. "Probably kept him from sending me into the rafters tonight."

"Probably did," I answered. "May have saved your life."

"Yup," Jessie agreed.

She gave Monty a couple of extra carrots that evening.

NAME CHANGE

I brought my new mare, Douceur (pronounced "Doo-sair," which means "Sweetness" in French) to Flying Horse Farm. Douceur stepped out of the trailer with her ears pricked and her head up, alert, but with the refined manners and dignity of a member of the nobility. A sober, female member of the nobility.

She entered her stall and examined each corner. After a few moments of dainty snuffling, Douceur nosed the hay in one corner and began meditatively chewing, still surveying her new home. I watched for a while.

Three of the Barn Chicklettes (as we call the high school girls who hang around the barn, riding and helping with chores and sometimes even doing their homework amid the friendly disarray in the viewing room) came over to meet Douceur.

"She's beautiful," said Faith.

"What's her name?" asked Amber.

"Douceur," I tried to say. It sounded much better when her previous owner, a Frenchwoman of great refinement, said it.

"Hey, Doos," said Amber to my new horse.

"She's beautiful," sighed Faith, again.

"Can I give her a treat?" asked Sophie.

"Sure," I answered. "In her bucket, though."

"Here, Doos," said Sophie.

"I think I'm going to change her name," I stated. The girls were shortening a beautiful name into something that sounded disturbingly like "doof" and that was not going to work.

"Call her Princess!" suggested Faith. "She looks like a princess."

"Or..." and I was inundated with names ranging from Disney characters to pop stars.

That night, I held an emergency meeting with Jessie, Francisca and Karen, who claims to be able to read a horse's ears to tell what they are really thinking. "Doos" was going to be something different by morning.

I said a proposed name, and Karen gave her verdict. If Douceur indicated it was OK, per Karen, Francisca and Jessie would each say it and Karen would tell us what Douceur thought of the name when said by others. None of the Disney princess names brought the desired ear reaction. Pop star names did not work. I was running out of ideas. I began trying random names.

"Juliette?" I tried Shakespeare. "Lady Macbeth? Ophelia? Desdemona?"

"Stop with the tragedies," suggested Jessie.

"Nancy? Fanny? Melissa? Lauren?" I continued. We were all getting tired of this game, and I was ready to call her "Horse" or "Mare."

"Celeste? Elizabeth? Beatrice?" I continued. Karen put up her hand.

"Stop there," Karen said.

I did, but began to comment. "It would be - " Just then Douceur nudged me, gently.

"Bea." said Karen. "Her ears like that."

"'Bea'?" asked Francisca. "It seems so plain!"

"Look at those ears," said Karen. "I tell ya, the ears never lie. She's picking that one."

Douceur's ears looked like she was paying attention to any chance of pocketed carrots, not so much to what people were saying, but "Bea" sounded fine to me, and it couldn't be shortened to something unfortunate.

"'Bea' it is," I announced.

"Shouldn't we break a bottle of champagne or something to christen her?" asked Francisca. Jessie laughed.

"No," said Jessie. "We'll each give her a carrot and a pat and then we'll go raid the soda machine."

And so we did. And "Douceur" became "Doos" became "Bea."

PHONE CALLS

Several months past, I had volunteered to take on simple office duties for the barn. My girlfriend, Shelly, had held this job to keep the costs of her horse habit down. Shelly had to move her attention to her ailing mother, and moved to another state to care for her. I took over her barn job, and I started getting the extra riding lessons that Shelly had been getting. After all, I was only going to return phone calls and schedule a few lessons in a calendar already too full to require much work. It'd be easy!

Right?

Wrong!

First of all, the number of calls seeking information that come into a barn are surprising, in more ways than one. And pretty much each question deserves a response:

"It says here on the web site that you offer riding lessons. Do you offer riding lessons?" asked the recorded voice. I called back. "Yes, we offer riding lessons," I said. "Thank you," the man said, and hung up. Nice talking with you, sir.

A call came in while I was checking messages, so I picked it up. "I'm selling a trough to hold water. In a field. For livestock. Horses are livestock," the caller said after brief greetings were exchanged. "Yes, ma'am, they are." "The water trough is seven feet long, two feet wide and two feet deep." "Thank you," I responded. "About the size of a coffin," the woman continued. "We're all set with water troughs," I told her. I wondered where she got her sales skills, but I didn't ask.

"I have a painting of a horse for sale," the message stated. "Call me if you're interested. It's very big." I did not return that call. I imagined a mural. The only painting the barn needs is on the shed out back. We're thinking white paint, again.

"I'm looking for a tour, on horseback. Do you give those?" No name, no phone number, no nothing. I wondered what he wanted to tour.

"Please call me at 555-1234. I want some information." Yes, ma'am, I want some information, too. I called and left a message that I had some information, and she should call me back with her questions. I tried to sound respectful and not sassy.

A recent favorite message stated, in a very plummy, expensive-sounding accent, "This is Renee. I am the personal assistant for Ms. Lily Pad (note: the names have been changed to protect my own personal behind). She is an experienced rider and interested in leasing a horse for weekly rides. Please return this call at 555-5678 and refer to matter number 4321." Huh? I actually know Lily, and I can imagine she has a personal assistant. She is a very successful designer, and her home decor items are fabulous (but would probably not work in my living room, which features an exercise ball and crafts from when my now-adult sons Bing and PJ were in pre-school). But does Lily really have so many tasks that they each require a four-digit reference number? Of course I returned the call, and found an agency that handles odd little tasks at the other end. Sort of a rent-a-wife, but that is too politically incorrect, so I can't call it that. Well, Lily didn't get a horse from us, because the barn owner doesn't willy-nilly believe that everyone who has a personal assistant who says she's an experienced rider truly is an experienced rider, and so we have a policy only to lease to lesson students. But I really, really want to hire one of these personal assistants to answer some of the phone messages I get...

REVENGE OF THE PHONE CALLS

Sales people call the barn phone asking to do surveys. In my job as Phone Answerer, Message Returner and Lesson Scheduler, I'd politely respond that I wasn't the owner, but would either answer the survey or alert the owner that her input was requested. The smart ones, or the ones experienced with Charleigh's attitude towards returning messages to answer surveys, just let me answer the questions. Charleigh, the owner, never responds to surveys unless there is a nice prize. Not the chance of a prize, and not some little one-serving sample of a wormer.

Charleigh doesn't do very many surveys.

But I do. The callers seem to have learned to take what they can get, which is me. Unfortunately for them, I am my father's daughter. He has made a retirement hobby out of amusing himself whenever he can. He wears the paper crowns distributed freely (mostly to children) at a fast-food restaurant whenever he goes there. He has driven an innocent woman (one of my in-laws) to within three steps of a madhouse by describing her indoor pool as an outdoor pool with the house wrapped around it (my mother had to shut him up, no easy task, or the outcome could have been serious). And he torments anyone who calls his home phone from a charity or a political party who asks for my mother by bellowing into the mouthpiece "She's supporting WHAT? I'll have to put a stop to THAT, by golly!" And heaven help the poor person who calls from a restricted number; Dad may have originated the prank of picking up a call from an phone number designated as "restricted," whispering "It's done, but there's blood everywhere" and hanging up.

So I come by this naturally.

I've returned every call that came into the barn, even the ones that asked if we did things that we don't do (like teach toddlers to ride miniature horses, or set up a trail ride ending with a catered luncheon in a gauze and flower-draped picnic shelter, with a discreet groom waiting to handle the horses while the riders have a romantic picnic - I am not making these requests up).

I'd try to find the callers an alternative if we did not provide what they wanted. But, sometimes, I crack.

"Do you have riding lessons? I want to learn to ride on a black horse," the message stated. It included a phone number. I returned the call. Yes, I told the nice lady who answered, we offer riding lessons. She repeated that she wanted to ride a black horse. We don't have any black lesson horses, and I know better than to promise a specific horse to anyone anyway. I assured her that we'd be able to teach her to ride a black horse by giving her lessons on a brown horse and having her wear dark sunglasses. She considered this. While she was thinking, I helpfully explained that we have a light grey horse, too, and we use different colored glasses to help people who wanted to learn to ride different colored horses. There was only a small extra fee for teaching students to ride specifically colored horses. She told me she'd get back to me.

I sincerely hope she doesn't. So do the instructors.

EVEN MORE PHONE CALLS

Sometimes it is difficult to understand - and to remember - family ties, what with blended families and multiple last names. At the barn where I ride, I also help with returning phone messages and scheduling lessons, special events and barn tours. Sometimes I get confused. One mother and daughter pair stand out particularly.

Zaghla, the mother, kept her maiden name for professional reasons (she is justifiably proud of her doctorate in a social science and her job as a high-level educator). Her daughter, Lilly M____, took her father's last name. When Zaghla left two messages on a particularly busy Saturday, they were separated by several other messages. I didn't recognize the number as the same. In one message, she was Zaghla P_____, calling about lessons for her unnamed daughter. In another message, two hours and seven other messages later, she was calling about lessons for Lilly M____.

I returned the first call and, with some effort, scheduled a lesson time that worked within the very narrow parameters set by Zaghla. Five calls later, I called Lilly M_____'s mother. Who was a very upset Zaghla. I had actually called her twice, and she was appalled.

She accused me, at great length, of being both unprofessional and a moron. I tucked my tongue firmly in my cheek and begged for forgiveness. I confessed my ignorance and humbly asked that she try to understand that I am new at this job. After a full minute and a half of apologizing (which is a very long time to grovel), Zaghla conceded that I shouldn't be executed.

I confessed to Charleigh, the barn's owner, who laughed.

"She's usually pretty nice to me," Charleigh said, and then grinned. "But I am important, because I own the barn. You are, of course, a minion."

"Please be kind to this lowly minion," I asked, "and bestow your forgiveness for my extremely unprofessional behavior."

Charleigh laughed some more. And she reported to me every time Zaghla did not bring her daughter to a scheduled lesson. We try to follow up on "no-shows" - they're a real problem, with a horse and an instructor waiting and the client usually unwilling to pay for a service they didn't get, not thinking that the lesson slot could have gone to someone else. Charleigh wouldn't let me follow up with Zaghla, though I did with everyone else.

Charleigh didn't want me to accuse Zaghla of being unprofessional. And Charleigh knows I would have. Happily.

TIME FOR A BARN IN MY BACKYARD

I board my mare. Bea lives in a lovely barn with other pleasure horses that occasionally go off the property to a show or a clinic or a trail ride. I've been happily going away with my husband for a few days, or sleeping in, or even congratulating myself for my generosity when I clean a stall or lug some hay bales "to help out." But something happened that changed my viewpoint. I want my own barn, in my backyard.

I slipped.

Happily wandering around the barn after working with Bea, I found the last remaining ice patch overlapping with the Northeast's infamous mud season. Mud season lasts roughly from "too icy to ride outside" season to "wow, we need more fly spray" season. Sometimes, like this year, the seasons run into each other.

Thanks to mud season, I landed softly. And squishily. In a particular type of mud that only horse facilities have. My left leg was soaked and covered with unmentionable substances. I tidied up as best I could in the barn. I had various cloths and sponges, but nothing really cleaned off the muck. I thought, briefly, of using the wash stall for a general hose off, but the weather was far from balmy - after all, there was still ice outside.

I'd planned on running errands on the way back from the barn. But not in these pants, not as they were now. The twelve miles between the barn and my house were lined with all the establishments I needed to visit that day. Frustrated, I spread a (relatively clean) towel on the car seat and gingerly levered my filthy self inside.

But there was a small second-hand store on the way home. One that catered to people of all walks of life, from the homeless looking for a warm jacket to the antique dealers looking for valuables that someone had carelessly donated. I decided to stop there, and get a cheap pair of (clean) pants. I parked, tied a sacrificial jacket around my waist to cover the worst of my pants, and strolled as casually and as rapidly as possible inside ("Smell? What smell? I don't smell anything - couldn't be my sodden pants!"). I found the rack of desperately cheap pants, and grabbed a pair of sweatpants from the rack labeled two sizes larger than my regular size and with an elastic waistband. I didn't look at them too closely; I didn't want to take any extra time in case my smell should catch up with me. I burned through the checkout line.

"Keep the change! I don't need a bag!" I sang out, gathering up the sweatpants and heading for the door. I clambered back into the car, the jacket around my waist now in roughly the same condition as my ruined pants, only on the inside. I drove to a remote part of the parking lot, far from other cars and any pedestrian pathways.

Having been to horse shows, I'd done this before. Any rider has. I slipped the seat as far back as it would go and arranged the clean sweatpants so that they'd be easy to get into quickly. I wiggled out of my disgusting pants and left them in a damp and reeking pile on the car floor. The sweatpants, of the nylon variety, should have slipped on easily. They did, over my feet. By the time I had pulled them up over my knees, I knew there was a problem. They'd been mislabeled. And they just didn't have enough stretch to make it all the way up my thighs and over my derriere. It would have to be a miracle fiber to do that, and it wasn't. It was nylon. Not even nylon knit.

I gave up. The sodden pile of old dirty pants wasn't going back on. I considered calling someone to rescue me. Rex, my husband, would have been greatly amused, but he wasn't available. He was at a club function, and there was no way I was going to call him there because he would have told every member of the Hartford Ski Club board that I was stuck in a parking lot in my cheetah boy-cut underpants. I tried one of my girlfriends, but when the call went to voicemail, I didn't leave a message. What would I say? "Hi, I am stuck in a parking lot in my underpants, can you please rescue me?" "I'm in my cheetah underpants and I need help because I fell in horse muck and the pants in the charity store were mislabeled." Nothing sounded quite right. I wished I'd made a better choice of underwear that morning, because that was what I was going to wear home.

I wadded up the dirty pants in the clean pants - everything was either getting a good washing when I got home or getting thrown out anyway - and arranged the jacket on my lap. So long as I didn't hit a stop light next to a truck or SUV or minivan - anything with a view into the driver's seat - and resisted drive-through coffee, and didn't speed or break any traffic laws, or run into a police inspection for seat belt use or drunk driving, I'd probably remain undiscovered. I pulled out of the parking lot, driving very carefully and well below the speed limit. Once I got home, I figured I'd be fine, so long as the carpenter who was fixing the wall in the bathroom wasn't there. I wasn't sure when he'd be by, and we'd known him for so long that we just gave him a key and let him handle things at his own pace. He gave us a good price in exchange for our accommodating attitude.

So I worried about Mr. Carpenter for about three miles, driving very carefully and slowly.

The odd "blurp" of a police siren startled me. He wanted me to pull over? Me, today, the cautious driver? Yes, indeedy, he did.

I pulled over and fiddled with the jacket. The police officer, a stereotype in mirrored sunglasses and a grim expression, strode to my window, which I opened.

"Hello, Officer," I said with a big smile to distract him from my bare calves and the distinct smell inside the car.

"Is everything OK, Ma'am?" he asked.

"Fine, Officer. Was I doing something wrong?"

"You were traveling pretty far under the speed limit. License and registration, please."

I reached to the glove box, where I keep my registration even though I've been told I'm not supposed to keep it there. My jacket slipped slightly. I felt it go, and hoped that my cheetah underpants weren't peeking out. I sat up straight, clutching a handful of papers from my glove box. I had every insurance card and registration form to hand from when I'd acquired the car. I shuffled them and scattered pieces all over my lap. My license was easier to find.

"Ma'am, is there a problem?"

I reached my limit. So far today I'd slipped and fallen in manure, bought pants that don't fit, and now was driving home in ugly underwear and was stopped by a cop for NOT SPEEDING. I took a deep breath.

And I told him.

"Look, I fell into mud made with unfortunate farm animal-type substances and ruined my pants, I tried to get replacements and they don't fit, I'm wearing my ugliest underwear under this jacket and maybe there is a contractor at my house who will be greatly amused when I walk in and NOW I'VE BEEN STOPPED FOR NOT SPEEDING. Yes, Officer, there is a problem."

The mirrored aviator sunglasses didn't waver, but the mouth beneath them lost its grimness and began to twitch.

"Leopard print isn't that ugly, Ma'am," he said.

I glared at him. That was unprofessional and ungentlemanly and no way to treat someone old enough to be his mother and I wanted his badge number. He took my license and registration. Before he returned, two other police cars had pulled up behind him and there was a little conference around the first car. They were laughing. Finally my original Stereotype Cop returned and handed me my license and papers.

"Hope your day improves, Ma'am," he said, mouth twitching.

I made it home and immediately packed a little bag with an emergency change of clothes, a washcloth and two towels and put it in my car.

And I did wish I'd gotten his badge number.

EPILOGUE

It's never the end. We all know that. So long as there are horses and the people who love them, and the people who love those people who love horses, or who know them, or have to interact with them after they've spent three hours cleaning horse things (like saddles or stalls or horses themselves) – anyway, there is no end. So laughing may make it easier.

Because if it is embarrassing or painful in any way, you can take comfort in knowing that, someday, it will make a good story.

Thank you for sharing these (entirely fictional) adventures – and if you'd like to share some of your own with me, please email me at carol.l.frey@gmail.com. And visit my website at www.carol-frey.com.

Carol Yingling

TO ANYONE WHO WILL LISTEN:

This is a work of fiction.

Sincerely,
Carol's husband
and
Carol's trainer

Praise for Carol Frey's
<u>Notes from The Domestic Underground</u>

The world is, indeed, a dangerous place. Hearts get broken. Entire governments tumble. The Atom Bomb lurks. The lintcatcher in the dryer catches on fire. A toilet explodes.

Carol Frey knows this world from down in the trenches, from the realest places there are: the kitchen floor with a filthy rag in her hand, the dinner table across from a glaring husband, the car full of screaming kids. It's perilous territory, this "domestic underground," and those trailblazers who've come before "Mama Bear" (Frey's nom-de-plume and alter ego) are no lot of shrinking violets— Erma Bombeck (whose *The Grass is Always Greener Over the Septic Tank* is the genre's bible), "Domestic Goddess" Roseanne Barr, Anne Taintor and her brilliant housewives-from-hell postcards, Phyllis Diller…the list goes on. Badass women all, they've been there, and lived to tell the dirty tale—laughing to keep from crying.

There's truth in every page here--and wit, and intelligence, and a big dose of common sense. Frey's "Mama Bear" has the kind of cherished perspective—truth-telling yet subtly sophisticated—that makes the world seem right, and places the really important things—family, friends, shoes, and cats—on the pedestals they deserve.

Christine Ohlman, The Beehive Queen
Singer/Songwriter

We all lead ordinary lives, filling our days and weeks with the routines and schedules that too often seem dull and uninteresting. We live for the extraordinary: the vacations, the holidays, perhaps a birthday or even just a "night out."

Not so Mama Bear, the alter ego of Carol Frey. With a keen eye, a sharp wit and a more-than-a-little-bent sense of humor, she lives the excitement, the humor and the love we sometimes wish we had more of in our lives. Come read, enjoy and experience a life, perhaps not so different from our own, but seeming so much more thrilling, adventuresome and outright funny.

Find in the antics of PJ, Bing and even Rex the children you have (or wish you had) and the husband you know too well (or are accused of being.)

Mama Bear has a "full" life and her stories will help fill yours with delightful reading you will enjoy from the first to the last page.

More importantly, her life will help you see your life differently, to see your ordinary as extraordinary, to enjoy your routines as holidays and your schedules as vacations where you find them.

Cheers to Carol Frey for sharing Mama Bear and her life with us. We can't wait to find out what happens next.

John Stewart, Amity Art Foundation

www.ingramcontent.com/pod-product-compliance
Lightning Source LLC
Chambersburg PA
CBHW061632040426
42446CB00010B/1383

**The Sign In
The Subway**